HOGMANAY
AND
TIFFANY

HOGMANAY
AND
TIFFANY

THE NAMES OF FEASTS AND FASTS

GILLIAN EDWARDS

Illustrated by Quentin Blake

GEOFFREY BLES · LONDON

Text © GILLIAN EDWARDS, 1970
Illustrations © GEOFFREY BLES LTD., 1970
SBN: 7138 0260 X

Printed in Great Britain
by Richard Clay (The Chaucer Press) Ltd
Bungay, Suffolk

Published by
GEOFFREY BLES LTD
52 Doughty Street, London, W.C.1
36-38 Clarence Street, Sydney 2000
353 Elizabeth Street, Melbourne, C.1
246 Queen Street, Brisbane
CML Building, King William Street, Adelaide
Lake Road, Northcote, Auckland
100 Lesmill Road, Don Mills, Ontario
P.O. Box 8879, Johannesburg
P.O. Box 834, Cape Town
P.O. Box 2800, Salisbury, Rhodesia

CONTENTS

I

FEASTS, FASTS AND HOLIDAYS

English is a patchwork quilt of a language. Over the centuries we have borrowed our words from Greek and Latin, from German, French and Italian, from Arabic, from Scandinavia, from Persia, Africa and India. The pattern they make is rich and scintillating, and they blend together so well we are seldom conscious of the ragbag beginnings of our English tongue.

Yet in some ways we remain insular, independent and different. This is particularly so in our Church Calendar. Though we at one time observed the same great feasts and fasts as other European nations our names for them are often unusual and sometimes unique. It is these names, their origins and their ramifications, that this book is all about.

The word fast itself we share with the Germanic languages. Ultimately it comes from an old Gothic *fastan*, meaning to hold fast, to keep or to guard. It was also used with the sense of keeping or observing a rule of some kind, of strict obedience to a law. To observe abstinence or to go without food was a specific application of this meaning, which in time became the commonly accepted one, so that to fast signified "to abstain from food as a religious observance or a ceremonial expression of grief". Fast as a noun covers both the act of fasting and the time or season at which it is proper to fast.

But a feast, "a religious anniversary appointed to be observed with rejoicing (hence opposed to a fast)", is French, not German. Once *feste*, it derives from Latin *festa*, festal or joyous ceremonies, religious in origin, since *festa* is related to *fanum*, meaning a temple. The Feasts of the Church were defined by a Catholic Dictionary in 1885 as "days on which the Church joyfully commemorates particular mysteries of the Christian religion or the glory of the saints."

The custom of observing saints' days seems to have begun from the practice of each local church in commemorating the *natalicia* of its bishops and more particularly its martyrs. These *natalicia* or birthdays were in fact death days on which fortunate and holy souls were born "into the higher life". Each church or group of churches drew up and maintained its own list. The earliest of these to have survived belongs to the local church of Rome. It is dated about 336 and notes twenty-four such commemorations, including Christmas, and with few exceptions all the entries appear in the Roman calendar of the present day. During the next hundred years the number of feasts had increased to a hundred and seventy, though a Carthaginian calendar mentions only seventy-nine.

Special prayers were said and lessons read on saints' days, and missals dating from the seventh and eighth centuries give these *Proprium de sanctis*, the prayers proper or appropriate to that day. Discovering what Mass to say became a difficult exercise, and missals and breviaries were provided with calendars listing the feasts and their appropriate dates. Such calendars are sometimes, even now, printed in Books of Common Prayer, and are of the perpetual variety, that is, "not for any special year but containing only the invariable elements common to all years, tables being given by which the movable feast days for any particular year may be ascertained." Movable feasts are those depending on the date of Easter, which is governed by the moon and has not yet been fixed, though it may be in time.

These early feast days, of course, meant more than hymn-singing and prayer. They were times of rejoicing and the people certainly rejoiced. After Mass came dancing and singing, games and sports, eating and drinking. Indeed the food and drink were so essential that at least from the twelfth century feast has had the secondary meaning of "a sumptuous meal or entertainment given to a number of guests, a banquet, especially of a more or less public nature." Though Christmas was, *par excellence*, the time for a feast of this kind, such a meal was not necessarily associated with a religious festival. Any pretext, in the Middle Ages, would do for those elaborate banquets they organised so well—a wedding, a christening, a tournament, an anniversary. But touches of their old character still clung, for they were almost always held in honour of something or someone and not simply as an excuse for having a good blow-out.

Soon, however, a feast became less formal and could be merely "an unusually abundant and delicious meal", even "something delicious to feed upon, a rich treat". And people began to talk about "a feast for the eyes" when they saw a beautiful landscape or "a feast for the ears" when they heard fine music, which is a long way from where the word began.

Meanwhile the abstemious ones were maintaining that all this gourmandising was unnecessary and injurious to the health. "When hunger is satisfied," noted Trusler in 1790, "even the sight of meat is disgusting—there is little difference between a feast and a bellyful." Similar sayings appear in many European languages; the observation seems to have been first made by Euripides about 421 B.C. In English its usual form is that recorded in 1562: "Folke saie, enough is as good as a feast."

A particular occasion of rejoicing was always the patronal festival or the feast of the saint to whom the parish church was dedicated. Every town and village held its own, known in France as the *fête du village*, in England as the village feast. There would be a church service, followed by sports and games, fireworks, perhaps a fair, and these celebrations continued long after saints' days ceased to be generally observed in this country. Usually, however, they were transferred to a Sunday, known as Feast Sunday or Hospital Sunday, money being collected for the local hospital. In this form they survived in some parts of England at least until the last war and may indeed still be held.

Nowadays, however, most churches and many other organisations give a fête, which is rather a different affair. *Fête* is merely the modern version of the Old French *feste*, re-borrowed in the eighteenth century when it became fashionable to adopt manners and expressions from abroad. Horace Walpole wrote in 1754 of a "great *fête* at St. Cloud", describing the kind of entertainment on a lavish scale, almost certainly out of doors, that the French court managed so superbly. Since then the word has firmly established itself in the English language, pronounced usually *fate* but sometimes *feet*, and signifying that most English of institutions, the garden party. Held determinedly outside or "if wet", which it usually is, "in the church hall", there are various stalls, displays of local talent, races, competitions, raffles, teas provided, and traditional side-shows such as Bingo, bowling for a pig, treasure hunts and hoop-la. It is still ostensibly "a gathering for pleasure", but we really go to part with our money in what we believe to be a worthy cause.

As the number of saints and thus of saints' days grew it became impossible to observe them all "with rejoicing" or no one would ever have done any work. By the Middle Ages feasts were graded in solemnity, and the more important ones indicated in ecclesiastical calendars with letters "made with red ink or with some red pigment". So Caxton observes in 1490, "we wryte yet in oure kalendars the hyghe festes wyth rede letters of colours of purpre". Purple was originally "any of various rich deep crimsons or scarlets", thus accounting for the confusion over the centuries regarding the colour of Cardinals' robes, which have always been red, even when described as purple.

These "hyghe festes" were the original "red letter days,
meaning important and memorable occasions, because the
major feasts were so marked." One fourteenth century calendar, indeed, goes even further, recording the so called greater
feasts not in red but in blue. Blue pigment at this time was
very highly priced; that is why, in medieval paintings, the
most important personages so often wear blue robes. In this
calendar, it is noted, "there were sixteen blue letter days and
sixty-two red letter ones; seventy-eight important feasts in
addition to Sundays, which helps to explain the slow growth
of productivity before the Reformation!"

After the Reformation the keeping of saints' days was
thought to be so typical of the Roman Church that Catholics
were known colloquially as "people of the Red Letter" or
"Red Letter men", which Grose defines in 1796 as "Roman
Catholics, from their observation of the saints' days marked
in red letters." Meanwhile the Church of England had long
abolished all festivals except the more important or red letter
ones from the calendar; those that remained were very much
joyful occasions, hence the use of the phrase to mean any
"especially fortunate or auspicious day in a person's life, or a
day to be remembered because of some important event or
benefit." Thus Coleridge in 1811: "To sit at the same table
with Grattan, who would not think it a memorable honour,
a red letter day in the almanac of his life?" And it is in this
sense, if at all, that we still use the phrase today.

Feast is, of course, a foreign borrowing. The English word
for "a day consecrated or set apart for religious observance,
usually in commemoration of some sacred person or event",
has been for a thousand years a *halig daeg* or holy day. In 1035
King Canute published a law *Be halidaeiges freolse*, glossed in
Latin as *De die dominica et festis observandis*, that is, concerning
the observation of Sundays and feasts. During the Middle Ages
this sometimes appears as two words—haly day, hooly day,

holy day—sometimes as one—haliday, holiday, and later with the modern pronunciation, holliday.

If the word had originally been a compound we would have expected it to keep its old sound and to be written haliday, on analogy with halibut and perhaps Halifax. The halibut or holibut is properly the *halig butt* or holy flat fish, so called "from being commonly eaten on holy days". Halifax is said by one authority to derive from *halig fleax* or holy flax field, by another from *halig feax* or holy hair, just as the surname Fairfax means fair-haired. This second tradition goes back to Camden who recorded about 1600, according to *Placenames of Yorkshire*, "a story of the maiden of Horton whose refusal to comply with the desires of a lustful priest led to her death at his hands; a tree on which her head was suspended became a holy resort of pilgrims; when the tree was finally stripped of its bark for relics, it was commonly believed that the fibres beneath the bark were the maiden's holy hair."

Unfortunately it now seems likely that *feax* here means coarse grass or even a wood (the "hair" of the fields), and that it was not holy at all, but *halh gefeaxe*, "an area of coarse grass in a loop of land or among rocks." None the less to most people whatever sounded like *hali* meant holy; Chaucer has the old form when he writes of how the parish clerk Absolon

> . . . that jolif was and gay,
> Gooth with a sencer on the haliday."

In time however *halig* changed to holi or holy and a new and later compound holiday came into use. It is interesting that as a surname, originally given perhaps as a baptismal name or as a nickname to "one born on a holy day", it survives in both forms, Halliday and Holliday.

A holy day was, of course, "a day on which ordinary occupations (of an individual or a community) are suspended, a day of exemption or cessation from work, a day of festivity, recreation or amusement", and by the middle of the sixteenth century, when the observation of feasts and saints' days had been almost entirely abolished, this had become its chief and almost its only meaning. In 1539 Taverner remarked, "with sluggers and unhardye persons, it is always holy days". And Googe in 1577, "Doo you not knowe that it is holliday, a day to dance in, and make merry at the Ale house?"

This sense of "cessation from work" accounts for an odd colloquial use of the word to signify "a spot left carelessly uncoated in tarring or painting". Grose noted in 1785, "A holiday is any part of a ship's bottom left uncovered in paying it", to pay here meaning to pitch. In Cornwall holidays were "parts left untouched in dusting", sweeping or cleaning; a maid would be adjured, "Don't leave any holidays."

The word retains its original sense only in the Roman Catholic church, which still has its Holidays of Obligation, "feast days on which Catholics are bound to assist at Mass and to refrain from servile work"—that is, all Sundays and about eight or ten other feasts. During the nineteenth century, perhaps under the influence of the Tractarian Movement, the spelling "holy day" was revived for use when the religious significance was specifically intended.

Nowadays, of course, there is nothing holy about our holiday or holidays, the first being collective, the second plural. They are firstly "a period of exemption from work granted to each employee of an industry or business, a leave of absence for rest and relaxation", and secondly that fortnight or so we spend beside the sea or in the country, on a cruise or just "abroad". Holidays with pay are a very modern institution, but as far back as 1573 Gabriel Harvey wrote of a friend, "In the hollidais he tooke a iurni into the cuntri". Stern types were indulging in walking tours by the eighteenth century; not till the nineteenth did the seaside become a fashionable and popular resort.

Holiday in this sense, writes Webster, is "chiefly British". We are almost the only nation to confuse our holidays with our feasts. In France in the summer they go *en vacance*, in Italy they have *le vacanze*, in Germany *Ferien*. Americans too have adopted the French word and speak of a vacation. This, as defined by the *Dictionary of American English*, is "a period of relaxation from one's customary occupation (= English holiday)".

Vacation is, of course, a perfectly good English word. Chaucer uses it. "Jankin oure clerk" spent his time reading his

> . . . book of wikked wyves
> When he had leyser and vacacioun
> From other worldly occupacioun.

That is, in his free time, his empty time, his *vacatio* or leisure, from Latin *vacare*, to be free from, empty, unoccupied. By the fifteenth century, however, it seems to have acquired the specific meaning of "a period during which there is a formal suspension of activity", and to be applied to that part of the year "during which law-courts, universities or schools are suspended or closed". Time stays, according to Shakespeare, "with lawiers in the vacation: for they sleepe between Terme and Terme". And in 1617 Moryson noted that lawyers "have their Termes to live in the City, and their Vacations to returne into the Countrey". With the same formality universities had their terms and their vacations; Milton while up at Cambridge wrote some lines to be recited "At a Vacation Exercise in the Colledge". To date this usage persists, though Vacation is in common speech generally known as "the Vac".

As for Bank Holidays, these are an entirely English institution. When the keeping of saints' days was abolished we were left with no public holidays, religious or otherwise, except perhaps for Christmas. Scrooge in 1843 complained of having to pay his clerk Cratchit "a day's wages for no work" on Christmas Day, in spite of the fact that "it was only once a year". Clearly this was the only time the poor clerk ever had off.

This situation caused much concern to a wealthy banker and scientist, Sir John Lubbock, M.P. for Maidstone from 1870 onwards. Employees in the Bank of England had been far better off than most workers, for the Bank was closed on "certain saints' days and anniversaries, to the number in all of about 33 days per annum". But in 1834, in true Scroogian manner, these holidays were reduced to four: Christmas Day, Good Friday, the first of May and the first of November (All Saints Day). The first two are, in fact, Bank Holidays under Common Law; that is, days on which the banks are always officially closed.

Sir John Lubbock proposed to extend the number of these holidays and to ensure they were observed by all banks. The result of his "unremitting zeal" was the passing in 1871 of "an Act to make provision for Bank Holidays", allowing for the closing of the Banks in England and Wales on Easter Monday, Whit Monday, the first Monday in August and Boxing Day, making with Christmas Day and Good Friday a total of six Bank Holidays in all. By the same Act, says the *Encyclopaedia Britannica*, "it was made lawful for the sovereign to appoint by proclamation any day to be observed as a bank holiday"—as was done at the Queen's Coronation—"or to substitute another day"—which Parliament has also done of recent years.

Although these were not statutory public holidays—they applied, as their name indicates, only to banks—they were observed almost from the passing of the Act by other employers, and workers tend to assume they are entitled to this time off with pay. But when the Act was first passed the holidays were a boon and a novelty to overworked, underpaid men. Their

appreciation, indeed, "was reflected in the temporary currency
of the term Saint Lubbock's Day for the first Monday in
August", later known as August Bank Holiday and now
metamorphosed into a movable feast, the Summer Bank
Holiday, which often falls in September. This, of course, is
quite as typically English as the Cambridge May Races which
are always held in June.

B

2

IN THE DISMAL

As well as feast days, medieval calendars included two days in each month which were believed to be extremely unlucky. On these days no business could be transacted; it was also very dangerous "to assault people . . . to drink, or eat, or to be bled". Popularly they were known as Egyptian days or *dies Aegyptiaci*, some say because they were first calculated by Egyptian astrologers, others because of some fanciful association "with the gloom of Egyptian darkness", when "there was a thick darkness in all the land of Egypt three days; they saw not one another, neither rose any from his place for three days." Perhaps the most common belief, however, connected them with the ten plagues called down by Moses upon the hard-hearted Pharaoh who would not let the Children of Israel go.

Certainly Egyptian astrologers, whose study of the stars was remarkably thorough and sophisticated, were accustomed to draw up lists of lucky and unlucky days according to the influence of the planets. Indeed they went further, classifying days as good, as prohibitive or purely bad, and those "on which there is a struggle in the world between good and evil". Moreover every day was further divided into three parts, each of which was subject to the influences having control at the time, so that what might be prohibited in the morning could be quite all right on the evening of the same day. Such careful calculators would never have declared particular dates to be permanently unlucky; everything depended on the position of the stars at a specific day and hour. None the less the tradition remained.

Vincent de Beauvais, a thirteenth century Dominican, tells in his *Speculum Majus* of these unlucky days: *In quodlibet mense sunt due dies, qui dicuntur Aegyptiaci, quorum unus est a principio mensis, alter a fine*—in each month there are two days, which are called Egyptian, one of which is at the beginning of the month, the other at the end. There are thus twenty-four such days in all, and he believes that they got their name from the plagues of Egypt, "which, as some said, took place on Egyptian days". The discrepancy in numbers is accounted for by the fact that Scripture only tells us of the more important sufferings inflicted on the unfortunate Egyptians; there were others, about which we have not been informed, "for it was asserted that there were minor plagues besides the ten." This opinion was shared by Bartolomaeus Anglicus in 1389: according to John of Trevisa's translation he maintained that "for there ben xxiiii Egypcyon dayes it folowyth that god sente mo wreches upon the Egypcyiouns than ten". If this were true they would certainly have cause to call these days unlucky.

Vincent de Beauvais goes on to explain how these dates were calculated—so many days from the beginning and so many from the end of each month. The actual dates usually given are as follows:

January 1 and 25;	February 4 and 26;
March 1 and 28;	April 10 and 20;
May 3 and 25;	June 10 and 16;
July 13 and 22;	August 1 and 30;
September 3 and 21;	October 3 and 22;
November 5 and 28;	December 7 and 22.

Rather strangely they are equally divided between odd and even dates. Among the Romans odd numbers were always lucky, even numbers unlucky; for this reason all their months had either thirty-one or twenty-nine days, except February, a time of penance and purification, with twenty-eight.

The only date we notice at once is November 5; perhaps poor Guy Fawkes should have taken warning. However, these were not all; according to Brewer, "the last Monday in April, the second Monday of August and the third Monday of December seem to have been specially baneful." An even worse day was Childermas or the feast of the Holy Innocents, December 28. It is said that when Edward IV learned this date had been chosen for his coronation he insisted that the ceremony should be postponed. As late as 1745 Swift could write, "Friday and Childermas are two cross days in the week, and it is impossible to have good luck on either of them." With all these unlucky days as well as feast days it seems a wonder any work got done at all. Friday, incidentally, does not seem to have been considered as expressly unlucky before the eighteenth century; why I do not know.

There was another and rather unexpected name for such unlucky days; what a fourteenth century writer refers to as "theis Egipcian daies (that we call dysmal)". And dismal is a fascinating word. Although it cannot be positively proved, most etymologists agree that it represents an Old French *dis mal*, which in turn comes from Latin *dies mali*, evil or unlucky days. Already, says Skeat, "in 1617 Minsheu derived it from 'Latin *dies malus*, an evill and unhappie time'." And he quotes two passages from an Anglo-French *Art de Kalendar* of 1256. Here the author writes of *jours denietz, Que vous dismal appelletz*—forbidden days, which you call dismal. And later, *Dismal les appelent plusours, Ceo est a dire les mals jours*—dismal several call them, that is to say the evil days.

Thus dismal was originally what the *OED* calls "a substantive of collective meaning" and in the Middle Ages was commonly used in some such phrase as "in the dismal" meaning "in the evil days" or "at an unlucky time". So Chaucer employs it in the *Book of the Duchesse*, where the knight, having

worshipped a lady from afar, described to the poet how at last
he plucked up his courage to tell her of his love:

> I not wel how that I began,
> Ful evel rehersen hit I can;
> And eek, as helpe me god with-al,
> I trowe hit was in the dismal,
> That was the ten woundes of Egipte,
> For many a word I over-skipte . . .
> I seyde, "Mercy!" and no more,
> Hit was no game, hit sat me sore.

By this, says Skeate, Chaucer means, "I think it must have
been in the evil days (i.e. on an unlucky day), such as were the
days of the ten plagues of Egypt." Plague, which we tend to
think of specifically as a malignant epidemic or pestilence, is
simply the Latin *plaga*, a stroke, blow, injury or disaster.
Chaucer chooses to translate it as "woundes", and it seems
clear from these lines that he "probably took dismal to be
derived from Old French *dismal*, i.e. ten evils."

It is scarcely surprising that "the consequence of proposing
on an unlucky day was a refusal". As the knight explains,

> God wot, she acounted not a stree
> Of al my tale, so thoghte me . . .
> I can not now wel counterfete
> Hir wordes, but this was the grete
> Of hir answere; she sayde, "nay",
> Al-outerly.

In time the original meaning of the word was forgotten.
It was thought to be an adjective, and people began to speak,
as Lydgate does in the fifteenth century, of dismal days: "Her
dismal daies and her fatal houres". The sense, however, had
not changed; Cranmer in 1548 roundly denounced those
foolish men who "thinke that when the Sonne, Moone, or any

other planete is in this or that signe, it is an unlucky thing to
enterprise this or that, and upon such dismolde daies (as they
call them) they will begin no new enterprise." Other church-
men joined him in condemning such superstitions. "Why,"
writes Bishop Pilkington, "shall we then be bolde to call them
evyll, infortunate and dismall dayes? Why should they not
prosper on those dayes as well as on other?" Yet there were still
many who maintained, with Neogeorgus, a sixteenth century
German Lutheran, on the subject of days, that

> Some of them Egyptian are, and full of jeopardee,
> And some again, beside the rest, both good and
> luckie be.

Astrologers from the beginning of time have been happy to
discover, for a fee, a fortunate day and hour for any enterprise.
Now they even tell us in our papers and magazines, free. And
a day when, as we say, the fates are against us, can be very
dismal indeed.

For by about 1600 dismal had almost entirely lost its connexion with days and was used as a general adjective, first with
the sense of "boding or bringing misfortune and disaster, unlucky, sinister, malign, fatal", and gradually weakening until
it implied merely "causing gloom or dejection, depressingly
dark, sombre, gloomy, dreary or cheerless." In eighteenth
century cant a "dismal ditty" was "the psalm sung by the
felons at the gallows, just before they are turned off". And in
the middle of the nineteenth century appeared the dismal
Jimmy, "a spoil sport, a wet blanket", a character very much
with us today.

Over the years too the word acquired other strange meanings.
It could signify the devil himself; so Levin in 1570 defines
"Ye dismall" as "devill, *diabolus*". In the eighteenth century
it was much associated with funerals, meaning mourning gar-
ments, particularly the deep black worn by widows, one such

being described as "decked out in her dismals", and also the black-costumed mutes engaged to follow a coffin—"Here is a whole pack of dismals coming to you with their black equipage". And ladies who suffered from those fashionable diseases "the spleen, the vapors, the horrors", might say they had "a fit of the dismals", that is low spirits or extreme dejection—rather what one feels when one stumbles and sprains one's ankle, breaks the best teapot, scalds the cat, spills tea on the carpet and exclaims, "This really isn't my lucky day!"

3
CHRISTMAS COMES

We are indeed a strange race. Four centuries ago the saying or even the hearing of Mass was made an illegal and treasonable act. Yet we are almost alone in calling "the Christian festival of the nativity" Christmas—the Mass or feast of Christ. Reformers many times have tried to abolish the celebration of Christmas, so far without success. It persists and so does its name, in spite of its blatant Popish associations—a name that has varied little over a thousand years.

It first appears as early as 1038 with the spelling Cristes Maesse. And according to the Chronicle for 1134, "This year heald se kyng Heanri his hird (court) aet Cristes maesse on Windlesoure (Windsor)." Cristes is the old genitive, so we have the meaning "Mass of Christ", the day on which it was proper for the Mass of the Nativity to be said. Moreover we have even kept the old pronunciation, for crist once rhymed with mist. Later the t became lost and the mass was slurred, so we arrive at our modern Crissmus, a sound which now needs a deliberate effort of mind to associate with Christ.

Mass itself, "the Roman Catholic celebration of the Eucharist", is a word with a long and disputed history. It is, says Skeat, "usually accounted for by supposing that the allusion is to the words ite, missa est (go, the congregation is dismissed), which were used at the conclusion of the service." This is far from being the only translation of ite, missa est; sufficient, however, that Latin missa with this sense of a form of worship occurs as early as the fourth century. Almost as early began the custom, unique in the calendar, of saying three Masses at Christmas, with three separate Propers or orders of service—one at midnight, one at dawn (the Aurora Mass) and a third somewhat later in the day.

The feast of the birthday of Christ is kept on December 25 throughout the Christian world. But this was not always so. In the primitive Church Epiphany, January 6, seems to have been celebrated instead. Even when the Nativity was recognised as a feast the chosen time varied locally, occurring in December, January or as late as March. Our modern date first appears in a Roman calendar of the year 336, where the entry for December 25 is *natus Cristus in Betleem Judeae*, and by the fifth century this observance had become general in the Western Church.

Since Saint Luke most remissly omits to tell us when Christ was actually born, all kinds of complicated calculations were indulged in by theologians; as they often started from different premises it is not surprising they seldom reached the same conclusion. One of the least abstruse was the belief that Christ was conceived on the same date as he died. The Crucifixion, it was decided, took place on March 25. Therefore Christ's conception or, as it is more generally known, the Annunciation, must also have been on March 25. Add on a logical nine months and the result is Christmas Day.

There were also two other results. First an approximation to the winter solstice, celebrated in Roman times from December 7 to 24 by the Saturnalia, "a period of general festivity, licence for slaves, giving of presents, lighting of candles", dressing up and merry making; and second, a co-incidence with the *dies natalis solis invicti* or the *sol novus*, the birthday of the unconquered sun, a Mithraic feast held at the time "when the victory of light over darkness begins to be apparent in the lengthening of the day", that is, about December 25. Some say these correspondences were accidental, some deliberate. Early Christian writers compare the *sol invictus* with the birth of the "Sun of Righteousness", but make no reference to the more riotous goings-on of the Saturnalia. Yet all these influences, together with those of other pagan winter festivals, survived and attached themselves to what became the English Christmas.

In a collection of proverbs dated 1573 we are admonished:

> At Christmas play and make good cheere,
> For Christmas comes but once a yeere.

'Thank God!' say many people nowadays. But when there was much less leisure and entertainment the feast was a landmark in the cold, dreary winter. "So long is Christmas cried that at length it comes," notes Cotgrave in 1611, translating the French saying, *Tant crie l'on Noel, qu'il vient.*

The old chroniclers always recorded where the King "kept his Christmas", and at one time the phrase was commonly used for observing "any similar festivity or revelry". Moreover Christmas applies not only to December 25; the word is "usually extended more or less vaguely to the season immediately preceding and following this day"—Christmas tide or Christmas time. Though the "twelve days of Christmas" are little more than a memory—except perhaps in a few ancient institutions like Trinity College, Cambridge, where the Statutes still provide that "during the Twelve Days of Christmas, wine, dessert and tobacco, including cigars and cigarettes, are free of charge to those taking wine in the Combination Room"—there yet remains a feeling that Christmas ends on Twelfth Day, January 6. Ecclesiastically, however, Christmastide lasts for several weeks; to be precise, until the Sunday called Septuagesima, "on any date between January 18 and February 22", according to when Easter Day falls.

It is in December that the holly and the mistletoe shine with their red and white berries. Unfortunately holly has no connexion with holy; its original form was *holen* or *holin*, and sometimes even *holme*. These and other evergreens were often known in dialect and nursery language as Christmas, from their close association with the feast. A glossary of 1825 defines Christmas as "the evergreens with which our churches and houses are still decorated at the season of Christmas". It is almost certainly a shortening of "Christmas decorations", to decorate meaning "to deck with ornamental accessories", from Latin *decorare*, to beautify, and related to decorum, that which is right and proper. "I must take down my Christmas," has a charming if melancholy sound.

To save time and space we often write Xmas for Christmas. To many people this seems a vulgarism, especially when pronounced *ex-muss*, but as a written form it is entirely respectable and has a long history. As Wyclif wrote about 1380, "X betokeneth Crist", and it was the common habit of scribes, before the days of printing, to substitute X or *Xp* for the name of Christ, either alone or in compounds. The *p* here stands for Greek *r*, so we get the famous *chi rho*, the symbol of Christ, the first two letters of Greek XPICTOC or *Khristos*. As early as 1100 we find the form "Xpes maesse", and a later spelling is "x'tenmass". Nowadays, however, apart from Xmas, we tend to an uneasy compromise between the English and the Greek; so bishops and other clergy often sign themselves "yours in Xt".

A child of either sex born on or about December 25 might well be given the name of Christmas. This is recorded from the thirteenth century, and still, though infrequently, persists. Perhaps the latest well-known person to bear it is Christmas Humphreys, barrister and author, and rather incongruously, a Buddhist convert. It also occurs as a surname, not unusual, along with Midwinter, which has much the same sense. For as well as signifying "the middle of winter, the winter solstice", it can sometimes mean Christmas itself, called in a tenth century manuscript "middeswintres maesse niht". This is confirmed by a sentence from one of John of Trevisa's translations, "Me schulde synge thre masses with *Gloria in excelsis* a mydwynter day", where the original has *in festo Natalis Domini.*

Today, however, a Christmas child is much more likely to be christened Noel, the French title for the feast. As a name it came to England along with the Normans or the Angevins; during the thirteenth century it was fairly common and gave rise to the surnames Noel and Nowell.

That there has always been this uncertainty in the spelling— it appears in French as *novel, noel* and even *noé*—has led some authors to identify it with *nouvelles,* news. The angel who appears to the shepherds brings them "glad tidings of great joy", *evangelizo gaudium magnum;* that is, the *god spel* or good tidings of our English Gospel. In an early play the angel is made to say:

> I come from hevin to tell
> The best nowellis that ever befell.

And in a more modern carol the singers cry 'News! News!' as if they were selling the evening paper. It seems, however, that there is confusion here rather than identity, and the repeated Nowells that we still sing at Christmas:

> Nowell sing we, both all and some,
> Now *Rex pacificus* is ycome,

may be merely an old shout of joy, reduced, they say, in some parts of England to 'Now well' or even 'No hell'.

Certainly the *OED*, while allowing that at one time Christmas was occasionally known as "the feste of nowel", gives only two meanings for this word in English—nowel, "a word shouted or sung as an expression of joy, originally to commemorate the birth of Christ", and noel, "a Christmas Carol". Grove elaborates on this; a noel is "a peculiar kind of hymn or canticle of medieval origin composed and sung in honour of the Nativity of Christ. The English Nowell or Novell was not confined to Christmas songs, but served as a general exclamation of joy." Formerly at the monastery of Angers in France "Noel . . . was sung fifteen times at the conclusion of lauds, during the eight days before the feast", and from this liturgical use it seems to have passed into general currency. Littré gives examples of occasions on which the cry was raised as *la naissance d'un prince, l'arrivée d'un soverain, etc.*

Basically, of course, Noel is the French word for the feast of the Nativity, and comes, as do similar words in all the Romance languages, even Welsh *Nadolig* and Gaelic *Nollaig*, from the Latin *natalis*. The full Latin name for Christmas is *festum nativitatis domini nostri Jesu Cristi*, the feast of the nativity of our Lord Jesus Christ, or in the more common shorter form *dies natalis domini*, the birthday of the Lord, with its remarkable resemblance to the old *dies natalis solis invicti*. From this comes, more obviously, the Italian *Natale*, the Spanish *Navidad* and the Portuguese *Natal*. The province of that name in South Africa was so called by Vasco da Gama, who discovered it on December 25, 1497. That the French version has lost its *t* is believed to be due to the barbarian Gauls who tended, like modern East Anglians, to swallow this letter when it came between two unstressed vowels. So for Latin *natalis* they said something like *na'al*, later softened to *noel*.

And from *dies natalis* comes a feminine Christian name Natalia or Natalie. Natalie is often met with in France and Germany, and sometimes occurs in England. With the Russians, including its charming diminutive Natasha, it is very popular and may have been re-borrowed from them by the French. Among the Orthodox, however, a child called Natalia is more likely to have been born on September 8 than at Christmas, for this is the feast-day of Saint Natalia, a lady well known in the East though not much regarded by the Western Church.

We have another surname associated with Christmas—Yule,

sometimes spelt Yull, Youle or Youell. It may once have been given as a font name; if so it has not survived, and in view of its expressly pagan connexions would doubtless have been unpopular with the Church. For Yule was "the name given . . . by the ancient Goths and Saxons to the festival of the winter solstice". In many parts of England and more particularly in Scotland though the feast was Christianised it still kept its old title, and even today it clings precariously to life.

Along with the name of Yule came many of its customs. Indeed it has been said that there is nothing specifically Christian about Christmas except the Mass and the adoration of the crib. The ritual of setting up in churches or in houses a model of the stable or cave where Christ was traditionally born is said to have been started by Saint Francis of Assisi. He wanted to bring home to contemporary Italy the poverty of the scene, to "represent as perfectly as possible the suffering and distress that he endured in his infancy to save us". Since then, unfortunately, cribs have become much more elaborate, with models of the Holy Family, the angels, the shepherds, the animals and the Kings, all richly dressed and looking remarkably clean and comfortable. But to see, as we sometimes still can, monks or nuns come in torchlight procession, singing and carrying the child, to place him in the manger at midnight on Christmas Eve is impressive and very moving.

All this to English and Scottish Puritans was sheer idolatry. No wonder they described Christmas as "anti-christ-Mass, abomination", as "the old Heathen's Feasting Day . . . the Papist's Massing Day . . . the superstitious Man's Idol Day, the Multitude's Idle Day". The feast, they said, was pagan and its celebration a sin. In 1647 all rejoicing was forbidden by Act of Parliament and in 1652 people were reminded that "no observance shall be had on the five-and-twentieth of December, commonly called Christmas Day; nor any solemnity used or exercised in churches in respect thereof." It

c

sounds very callous and hard, but since most authorities agree that Christmas as Europe observed it was a strange uneasy combination of "the Saturnalia, with its freedom, its levelling of rank and age, and its making light of tradition", and "the Yule celebration, which was essentially a feast of the dark ancestral spirits", it may be conceded that these divines did have a point. Even our present-giving dates back to the Saturnalia, when "all classes exchanged gifts, the commonest being wax tapers and clay dolls".

The Yule feast of northern Europe, says the *Dictionary of Folklore*, was "a solstice observance celebrating the lengthening of the day with the return of the sun and concerning itself principally with the spirits of the dead". It was also, according to the *Encyclopaedia of Religion*, the time of the *julblot* or midwinter sacrifice "for a good crop, for the year's luck and for peace". This sacrifice offered to Frey, "the god to be invoked for fertility and peace", was usually a pig, called the *julgalt*. Some see in the Boar's Head, that dish once essential to a Christmas feast, a survival of this custom.

Not only gods but spirits had to be appeased. At this time of the year the nights were long and dark, especially in the northern countries. Monsters and evil demons roamed the earth, and in the storm could be heard the shouts and cries of the Wild Hunt, the Asgardsreid, devils pursuing souls. Gentler ghosts were also abroad, for members of families lately dead returned to visit their old homes. On Christmas Eve houses were prepared for guests, swept and polished and a meal left ready on the table. While everyone went to Midnight Mass the dead came to see all was in order, and sat down and feasted themselves on "the immaterial part" of the food. Perhaps this is the origin of our persistent belief that Christmas is the time for ghosts and for our "notion of houses being haunted by . . . their former occupants".

Indeed the word Yule has something ghostly about it.

Although it was used for the time of the midwinter solstice, and later and more especially for Christmastide—"Crist wass borenn i this life withinnen yoless moneth"—no one knows exactly what it meant or how it was derived. It is clearly re-lated to Old Norse *jol*, "a heathen feast lasting twelve days", to Danish *juul* and Swedish *jul*, which have also come to mean Christmas, and must go back to some far more ancient origin, Gothic perhaps.

In English it appears very early, with the spelling *geohol* or *geol*. A writer about 900, trying to explain its occurrence in the Calendar, makes it sound rather like "jam tomorrow and jam yesterday—but never jam today". For, he says, the month of December "is named *Decembris* in Latin, and in our tongue the former Yule, because two months are named with one name; one is the former Yule (*se aerra geola*) the other the after Yule (*se aeftera geola*) because one of them comes before the sun, *viz.* before it turns itself about (at the winter solstice) to the lengthening of the day, whilst the other (January) comes after." Bede gives the same account in Latin, but he calls the two months *Januarius, dicitur Giuli* and *December Giuli*, that is December and January of Yule. This spelling *Giulus* some connect with Old Norse *ylir*, "the month beginning on the second day of the week falling within November 10 to 17", or with the Gothic name for November, *fruma jiuleis*, said to mean the first Yule; "a name not necessarily inconsistent with the Anglo-Saxon use, since November may once have been reckoned as a Yule-month." From this it seems that Yule was both a season and a feast, but which took its name from the other we cannot be sure.

By the Middle Ages, however, "the feste of yole" was firmly established as Christmas, chiefly from the coincidence of the time. And with its heathen name it took on the pagan trappings of the Saturnalia. "At Ewle we wonten, gambole, daunce, to carole and to sing," said a writer in 1589. By 1661 Fuller was maintaining that "Yule is a name general for festivals", although it does not appear that he was right. Indeed its use was already dying, though in Scotland it survived much longer. Sir Walter Scott quite naturally makes one of his characters say, "It cam a green Yule, and the folk died thick and fast; for ye ken a green Yule makes a fat kirkyard." Perhaps through his influence it then re-appeared in England as what the *OED* calls "a literary archaism", putting the blame, apparently, on Tennyson, who heard, in *In Memoriam*,

> The Christmas bells from hill to hill
> Answer each other in the mist . . .
> The merry merry bells of Yule.

The spelling Ewle, by the way, is aberrant. The town of that name, Ewell in *Surrey*, has no connexion with Christmas; it means the source of a river, a spring from which a stream flows, in Anglo-Saxon *aewiell*.

Enterprising etymologists, professional and amateur, have had great fun with this word. "Some," says Northall in his *English Folk-rhymes*, "maintain it to be derived from the Greek *oelos* or *ioelos*, the name of a hymn in honour of Ceres, others say it comes from the Latin *jubilum*, signifying a time of rejoicing, or from its being a festival in honour of Julius Caesar; whilst some also explain its meaning as synonymous with *ol* or *oel*, which in the ancient Gothic language denotes a feast, and also the favourite liquor used on such occasions whence our word ale."

Another explanation connects it with Gothic *giul* or *hiul*, Anglo-Saxon *hweol* and our wheel, on the ground that Yule was "the turning-point of the year, or the period at which the fiery orb of day made a revolution in his usual circuit and entered on his northern journey." This view appears to be confirmed "by the circumstance that, in the old clog almanacs, a wheel is the device employed for marking the season of

yuletide". There is nothing so deceiving as coincidence; this
reasoning may well be *a posteriori*. Skeat calls it far-fetched,
insists the spelling is all against it, and points out that "Yule
did not denote the shortest day, but a season".

Others have gone further afield. C. M. Yonge suggests it
might "perhaps be traced in the Persian *giulous*, the anniversary
of a coronation". Lehmann, mindful of the returning dead,
says it has been "derived distantly from Sanskrit *yaic*, to invite
(invitation of guests or ghosts?)". And Eric Partridge enters
the fray "very tentatively indeed" with the proposition that
geol may derive from an earlier *geul*, a form of Latin *gelu*,
meaning cold. Thus *"geola*, December, is, in the Northern
Hemisphere, a month notoriously cold, with *geol*, Yule,
falling in what is usually its coldest period; the cold month
and the festival—the most important day—of the cold season".
This is ingenious but begs any number of questions, not the
least than in England January on the whole is much colder
than December.

> The blackest month in all the year
> Is the month of Janiveer,

while December is merely "dirty".

From these speculations the *OED* keeps aloof, saying merely
that "the ultimate origin is obscure". But it does allow that
there may be a possible connexion between Yule or *jol* and our
word jolly. In its original form *jolif* we borrowed it from
French, and it once meant "iollie, pleasant, ioyous, blithe,
bonnie, buckesome". If it comes from *jol* its chief sense may
have been festive, though some prefer to relate it to Latin
gaudius, from *gaudere*, to rejoice, as when "gaudye days" used
to be days of feasting. So perhaps we should wish each other,
instead of "A merry Christmas", "A jolly Yule".

Certainly Yule, like Noel, was once "used as an exclamation
of joy or revelry at the Christmas festivities". Blount recorded

in 1661 how "in Yorkshire and our other northern parts, they have an old Custom, after Sermon or Service on Christmas Day, the people will, even in the churches, cry Vle, Vle, Vle . . . and the common people run about the streets singing

> Ule, Ule, Ule,
> Three Puddings in a Pule,
> Crack nuts and cry Ule."

(A pule was a pillow, so perhaps a bag for cooking the puddings in.)

A pity we have lost the custom; it could liven things up a bit. But then we might be arrested like poor "Wm. Bell, baxter", who in 1574 was brought before the Kirk Session because "in his hous (at Christmas), the same being ful of lychtis and mony in company, hymself cryit wyth lowd voice superstitiously, 'Zuil! Zuil! Zuil!'." There was indeed a cynical proverb current, at least from the sixteenth century, that "it is easy to cry Ule at other men's coste".

Another piece of wisdom, also Scottish, tells us

> He is a fool
> That marries his wife at Yule,
> For when the corn's to shear
> The bairn's to bear.

This was, of course, before the time of the pill, and is thus explained by Kelly: "If a woman be got with child at Christmas, it is like that she may lye in harvest, the throngest (busiest) time of the year." Another saying, in the nature of meaningless repartee, was "Now is now, and Yule's in winter", which Kelly again interprets as "a return to them that say *Now*, by way of resentment; a particle common in Scotland."

Perhaps the chief attribute of Yule we remember, rather nostalgically today when so many never see a living fire, is the Yule-log. "I am apt to believe," says Bourne, "the log has the name of the Yule-log from its being burnt as an emblem of the returning sun", and there seems little doubt that this is true. The log itself was "as large a piece of wood as could be conveniently burned" in the hearth; sometimes it consisted of "the root of a large tree together with the lowest part of the trunk". It was brought in with much ceremony on Christmas Eve, solemnly lit, and "allowed to burn for at least twelve hours, if ill-luck was to be averted". The log became endowed "with sacred and occult properties", and many customs and omens were associated with it.

Moreover it had many names. Sometimes it was called the Yule-clog, a clog being a block of wood. It was also the Christmas log and the Christmas braun or brand. In Gaelic it became the *Cailleach Nollich*, the Old Woman of Christmas; in France the *bûche de noel*. Even in Italy they have what they call the *ceppo*, the bole or trunk of a tree. Because the *Ceppo* is or was burnt on the hearth at Christmas, it gave its name to a party or present or even the feast itself, *Il Ceppo*, carrying us back to its old symbolism of fire and the unconquered sun.

4

PRAY, SIR, REMEMBER THE BOX

When that notable monarch "good King Wenceslas" set out with his page to take meat and drink and pine logs to a poor man he may have been following "a custom, ancient and still extant, of giving and receiving presents, usually money and articles of personal wear, on the day of Saint Stephen." But though we sing about it few English people know "the feast of Stephen", the Jewish protomartyr, falls on December 26. True to our commercial instinct we call it Boxing Day.

The name itself does not seem to be very old, dating perhaps from the eighteenth or nineteenth centuries; the practice it commemorates, however, goes back for hundreds of years. The *OED*'s first mention is from Soane, who wrote in 1849, "the feast of Saint Stephen is more generally known amongst us as Boxing-day", while a Lincolnshire Glossary defines Boxing-time as "any time between Christmas Day and the end of the first week in January". Having got hold of the name, a writer in *Harper's Magazine* tried to explain it in 1884 by saying "in consequence of the multiplicity of business on Christmas-day, the giving of Christmas-boxes was postponed to the 26th . . . which became the established Boxing-Day, sometimes known as Box-day." He has the right idea but gets the cart before the horse, since Christmas boxes are not, strictly speaking, Christmas presents at all. They are receptacles in which money was collected.

One meaning of box has always been a "money-box, containing either private or public funds, often with a defining word added"; for example the poor-box, in which money for the poor was put. Attempts to give Boxing Day a religious origin associate it with such alms-boxes, usually made of wood with strong iron locks and padlocks, and kept in churches. Thus Brewer says, "Boxes placed in Churches for casual offerings used to be opened on Christmas Day, and the contents, called 'the dole of the Christmas Box', or the 'box-money', were distributed next day by the priests." Or again, according to William Sandys, "Some have derived the Christmas Box from the practice of the monks to offer masses for the safety of all the vessels that went long voyages, in each of which a box, under the control of the priest, was kept for offerings; this was opened at Christmas, whence the name arose." However he goes on to add that "this does not seem a probable derivation", and no evidence has been produced for either of these practices.

It is certainly true that Boxing Day was also called Offering Day, "as Christmas boxes are said to have been religious gifts", and the 1548 Book of Common Prayer has a rubric stating that "at the offerying daies appoynted every manne and woman shall paie to the Curate the due and accustomed offerynge." But these were to be collected "in a decent bason" rather than a box, and there is no special reference to Christmas. Moreover as early as 1440 an "offeryng" was defined as "a present to a lorde at Crystemasse or other tymys", which would seem to make it remarkably secular.

And secular the Christmas box proper certainly was. Johnson called it "a little box in which little presents are collected at Christmas." This is vague and not entirely correct. Cotgrave in 1611, translating the French *tirelire*, gives us the best description: "A Christmas box: a box having a cleft on the lid, or in the side, for money to enter it; used in France by begging Fryers, and here by Butlers and Prentices, etc." Even he omits the essential characteristic that though money could be put in through the slot it could not be got out; the only way to empty the box was to break it.

Tirelire in French again has no connexion with Christmas;

it means simply this kind of a box, having *une fente par où l'on fait entrer des pièces de monnaie, sans pouvoir les retirer autrement qu'en brisant la tirelire.* This charming word has been derived from Italian *tirare*, to take out or extract, and *lire*, coins; but, says Littré, it is not Italian, for in Italy such a box is known as *un salvadenaio*, a money-saver. *Tirelire* is merely *un mot de fantasie.*[1]

These, then, were the kind of boxes in which, about the sixteenth century, apprentices began to collect money at Christmas from their masters' customers, as well as "journeymen and the servants even of the higher classes, such as butlers of the Inns of Court". Pepys, in 1668, having been "called up (on December 28) by drums and trumpets" complained that "these things and boxes (have) cost me much money this Christmas". A box by definition is, "unless otherwise specified, understood to be four-sided and made of wood", and by derivation specifically something of *buxum*, box-wood, the wood of the box-tree. But Christmas boxes were almost always made of earthenware, manufactured *ad hoc* and used on one occasion only. Once the collection was complete there would be, no doubt, a ceremonial smashing in the presence of all those, whether servants or apprentices, who stood to benefit. The money would then be shared out and spent perhaps on having a "smashing" time.

The great advantage, of course, of these containers was that no one could cheat by helping himself to the contents when the others weren't looking. So common were such boxes in the seventeenth century that casual reference is often made to them. Thus Mason, writing in 1621 of a grasping man, says, "As an apprentices' box of earth, apt he is to take all but to restore none till he be broken." And Bishop Hall, a little earlier, remarked even more pointedly, "It is a shame for

[1] It may, in fact, be part of the refrain of an old song, the same "Tirra lirra" that "by the river sang Sir Lancelot". See p. 177 below.

a rich Christian to be like a Christmas box, that receives all, and nothing can be got out till it be broken in pieces."

According to Fr. Weisner, "a similar custom prevailed in Holland and some parts of Germany, where children were taught to save their pennies in a pig-shaped earthenware box. This box was not to be opened until Christmas and consequently was called the 'feast pig'." Could this, one wonders, have some remote connexion with the *julgalt*, the pig sacrificed to Frey at the feast of Yule? Or is it simply that the pig in Germany is a symbol of prosperity and good luck?

Certainly this must be the origin of our china or pottery "piggy banks" which have become so popular of recent years. The custom was probably taken by emigrants to America and thence came back to us. For although later editions of Webster include the word piggy-bank—"a bank often in the shape of a pig and usually used by children for saving small coins"—it does not yet seem to have found its way into English dictionaries. It is, however, interesting to note that in earlier times a pig was the name of "an earthenware pot, pitcher, jar or other vessel", and a piggy "a little pot". Moreover pig could also mean a sixpence; if one kept one's pigs in a piggy the effect would be the same as having a piggy-bank.

Indeed if Aubrey can be believed, which isn't always the case, the Romans themselves had pottery money boxes. For he recorded the finding, about 1670, in Wiltshire of a Roman hoard which included "an earthen pott of the colour of a Crucible, and of the shape of a prentices' Christmas Box, with a slit in it, containing about a quart, which was near full of money."

Sandys notes that servants and butlers also had their boxes. This was particularly so in the gaming clubs that flourished during the seventeenth and eighteenth centuries. Here appeared what was known as the Butler's Box, "a box into which players put a portion of their winnings at Christmas time as a

'Christmas-box' for the butler." It was, of course, to the butler they would call for wine to wet their anxious throats. His very name, sometimes spelt *bottelar*, comes from French *bouteillier*, derived in its turn from *bouteille*, a bottle. From the days when his position was a lordly one, that of "officer in charge of wine for the royal table", his job has always been to supervise the cellar and keep the glasses filled.

It seems he must have done quite well from the contents of his box, for that too became almost proverbial, especially as a comparison for lawyers and the law. "Westminster Hall", said Taylor in 1629, "is like a Butler's Box at Christmas among the gamesters: for whosoever loseth, the Box will bee sure to bee a winner." And again, a little earlier, in a *Tract Against Usurie*, "the old Comparison, which compares usury to the butler's boxe, deserves to be remembered. Whilst men are at play, they feele not what they give to the boxe, but at the end of Christmas it makes all or neere gamesters losers."

In time other functionaries began to think some recognition of their services was due to them at Christmas. Steele, in 1712, complains, in the character of Hezekiah Thrift, of the abominable state of the Royal Exchange, on account of "the Walnut Trade carry'd on by old Women within the Walks, which makes the Place impassable by reason of Shells and Trash. The Benches around are so filthy, that no-one can sit down, yet the Beadles and Officers have the Impudence at Christmas to ask for their Box, tho' they deserve the Strapado." Box here has come to mean the sum of money such officials expect, what the *OED* calls "a present or gratuity given at Christmas", and it is in this sense we continue to use the word.

At the end of last century, when the *OED* was compiled, these Christmas boxes were "usually confined to gratuities given to those who are supposed to have a vague claim upon the donor for services rendered to him as one of the general public by whom they are employed and paid, or as a customer or their legal employer; the undefined theory being that as they have done offices for this person, for which he has not directly paid them, some direct acknowledgement is becoming at Christmas. Thus these gratuities are asked from householders by letter-carriers, policemen, lamp-lighters, scavengers, butchers' and bakers' boys, tradesmen's carmen, etc., and from tradesmen by the servants of households that deal with them, etc."

Times have changed since then, yet many people, among them the "scavengers", still feel they have a "vague claim" on our generosity at Christmas. As for the "letter-carriers", when in 1880 the Post Office was establishing free and regular deliveries of mail to all households they carefully explained that though "no payment in addition to postage" should be made, this prohibition "does not, however, extend to Christmas boxes".

Eventually the box and its association with Boxing Day were forgotten; those who now expect gratuities think they should come before Christmas, not after. So the Christmas box is becoming more and more "the popular name for the Christmas present, whether money, books, gloves, chocolate or other articles". To the compilers of the *OED* this use was "vulgar". But the habit of the box, if it may be so called, has not entirely disappeared. As late as 1814 it was recorded from Yorkshire that "in the barbers' shops a thrift box is put by the apprentices against the wall to receive donations from customers." Even today in the middle of December decorated boxes or tins may appear in restaurants, supermarkets or the like, inviting contributions for the staff. And long ago certain charities had a similar idea; their collecting boxes, carefully sealed with labels, are almost impossible to open unless these are torn off.

Scotland, however, observed its own feast, Handsel Monday,

though Burton noted sadly in 1864 that "the handsel . . . has fallen into disuse, having been superseded by that great institution, the Box-day." This handsel was a present, usually of money, given to servants and children, on Handsel Monday, "the first Monday of the year, so called because it has been the custom, from time immemorial, for servants and others to ask or receive handsel on this day." Certainly the practice, if not the word itself, which was noted as "ancient" in 1657, may go right back to Roman times. For Cotgrave in 1611 translated the French *estrener* as "to handsell or bestow a New-yeares gift on". *Etrenne*, meaning a New Year's gift, has had at various times all the senses of English handsel, yet comes direct from Latin *strena*, a present given at New Year.

Handsel, which in nineteenth century Scotland had become not a friendly gift but "a kind of wage still expected and received by those in service", was a very different thing from the casual contributions that went into the Christmas box. The word, which is Scandinavian in origin, had a long career in English and has only recently died. Skeat derives it from Icelandic *hand* and *sal*, a sale or bargain, *handsal* being an ancient law term for "the transaction of a bargain by joining hands". For as he explains, "hand shaking was with the men of old the sign of a transaction, and is still used among farmers and the like, so that to shake hands is the same as to conclude a bargain." "Shake on it" we sometimes say even now when we settle an agreement or dispute.

In a glossary of 1053, however, the Anglo-Saxon *handselen* is given as the equivalent of Latin *mancipatio*, "giving into the hands of another". *Mancipium*, from *manus* and *capere*, a taking in hand, was "an old form of sale and purchase in Rome"; it was also "a slave acquired by this process", and turned into the English manciple, a kind of steward whose job it was to buy provisions.

At this point one gaily remembers the Italian *mancia*, a tip, a gift, a *pourboire*, borrowed by the French as *manche*, with the same meaning. Alas, the trail is false, though none the less interesting. For *mancia* has no relation to *mancipatio* except by confusion; *manche* in French is a sleeve, so *mancia* should really be *manica*. Its unexpected secondary sense of a free gift or present dates back, says Battisti, to the days of chivalry, when at tournaments the lady gave her chosen knight a token to wear in his helm as he fought, which token was usually a scarf or a *manica*, a long loose sleeve.

To return to *handselen*, its primary meaning would seem to be "delivery into the hand or hand-gift". What was delivered was often the payment of a first instalment of the promised money, what we would call a deposit or an advance put down "to secure the goods". Thus, says Skeat, "it was formerly usual in making a bargain to pay a small part of the price at once, to conclude the bargain and as an earnest of the rest." Moreover handsel brought good luck. From the point of view of the seller rather than the buyer it came to mean the first money taken over the counter in the morning, which was looked on as some kind of omen or augury. "It is a common practice," wrote Grose in 1787, "among the lower class of hucksters, pedlars or dealers, on receiving the price of the first goods sold that day, which they called handsel, to spit on the money, as they term it, for good luck."

This sense of a payment or present to bring good luck on a first occasion runs through all the uses of handsel. Such a gift might be offered when friends or neighbours "entered upon any new condition, situation or circumstances", when they moved to a new house, or even when they first put on new clothes. Just as the Roman *strenae* brought good fortune for the coming year, so the handsel ensured good luck to any new venture. That the customs of Handsel Monday sprang from this belief is confirmed by a writer in 1657 who notes, "the first day of this yeir . . . the pepill observit the old ancient, bot beggarlie, custom, in seeking, craving and begging handsell; many superstituouslie believing that thai could not thryve all that yeir except thai haid gotten a New Yeir's gift."

It was not only servants and children who expected handsel. A Scottish Statistical Account for 1793 records that "besides the stated fees the master (of the parochial school) receives some small gratuity, generally 2d or 3d, from each scholar on handsel Monday." A gratuity is a free gift, something *gratuitus*, freely given. But this money, like most gratuities, seems to have been more or less compulsory. "Scholars," we learn, "commonly give a handsel to their master or mistress on this day. The boy who gives the largest sum is called the king, and the girl the queen, and the king claims the right of demanding at least that day as a holiday." This seems an unexpected proceeding for democratic Scotland, yet it has strange echoes of the Bean-king and his queen who ruled at the Twelfth Night feast.

Nor were the children alone in being able to enjoy themselves, for "it is well known that the first Monday of the year is always observed with uncommon Gaiety and Mirth and in Consequence becomes a Holiday to Apprentices and Servants." And if one of them should happen to be the first customer in the bar he might get, for handsel, a free drink "on the house".

D

5

MINC'D PIES AND PLUM-PORRIDGE

Now thrice welcome Christmas,
Which brings us good cheer,
Minc'd pies and plum-porridge,
Good ale and strong beer.

So proclaims *Poor Robin's Almanack* for 1695. Plum-porridge or plum-pottage may not sound to us very inviting, but "in old times (it) was always served with the first course of a Christmas dinner." The recipe can be found in a cookery book of 1713: "To make plumb-broth—Take a leg of beef, and a piece of the neck . . . two pound of currans . . . three pound of raisins of the sun, three pound prunes well stew'd . . . have a two-penny white loaf grated, mix it with some of the broth, and put the pulp into it . . . garnish the dish with some of the stew'd prunes, some raisins and currans out of the broth." Spices were also added, cloves, mace and ginger, and sometimes wine and sugar; a strange conglomeration of sweet and savoury, almost a dinner in itself. Nowadays we prefer our plum-pudding, though we still enjoy mince-pies.

Puddings and pies are typically English dishes, and both are almost exclusively English words. A pie, of course, is quite a simple thing, "a dish composed of meat, fowl, fish, fruit or vegetables, etc., enclosed in or covered with a layer of paste and baked." Other countries have them but tend to call them pasties, *pâté* or *pasticcio*, because they are covered with paste. The *OED* states categorically that "no related word is known outside English except Gaelic *pighe*", and that was clearly borrowed from Lowland Scots.

Yet pies have been pies in England since at least the thirteenth century. They first appear in the accounts of Bolton Priory for 1303, intruding into the learned Latin; during that year nine quarters one bushel of wheat were provided for use *in pane . . . et in pyis et pastellis*, in bread, in pies and pasties. By Langland's time "cokes and here knaves" stood outside their shops touting for custom, crying "hote pies, hote!", while the taverners joined in with

> White wyn of Oseye and red wyn of Gascoigne,
> Of the Ryne and of the Rochel.

And Chaucer's Cook, an expert in his trade, "coude roste and sethe and broille and frye . . . and wel bake a pie."

Such pies contained meat or fish. A fifteenth century recipe for "pyez de parez" or Paris pies begins, "Take and smyte fayre buttys of Porke, and buttys Vele, to-gederys". By 1706, however, Phillips could say, "Pie, a well-known Dish of Meat or Fruit bak'd in Paste". And the earliest fruit that found its way into a pie seems to have been an apple; in 1590 Robert Greene charmingly wrote to a lady, "Thy breath is like the steam of apple-pyes".

The pastry crust was usually made of flour and water, sometimes with the addition of eggs. "Make a fayre past", the medieval cook was instructed, "of flowre and water, sugre, and Safroun, and Salt; and then make fayre round cofyns ther-of." This word coffin, in early times the common term for a pie-crust, comes from the Latin *cophinus* and once meant "a baskette . . . made of wyckers or bull rushes, or barke of a tree: such oone was Moyses put in to." Later it had the added sense of a chest, casket or box, and was used to describe both pie-crust and "the chest in which a corpse is buried". Having acquired this unpleasant association it lost its other meanings.

How our word pie originated nobody can be sure. Since pie,

from Latin *pica*, was used very early for a magpie (called at one time a maggot-pie or Margaret pie), etymologists have sought for a connexion, but so far one hasn't been proved. Skeat suggests "the miscellaneous nature of the dish's contents might recall the black and white or piebald appearance of the bird". Partridge wonders if perhaps it was "originally made with magpies"; this seems a little too obvious to be true. Or again the name may be merely "a medieval pleasantry", comparing the varied collection of ingredients necessary with "the habit which the magpie has of picking up and forming accumulations of miscellaneous articles."

Two other parallel words surprisingly support this derivation. One is chewet, formerly used for a small meat pie and apparently identical with French *chouette*, now meaning an owl but once the name for "a chough, cadesse, daw, jackdaw". The other, even more unexpected, is haggis, another dish of miscellaneous content, which some compare with the old English word for a magpie, haggess. This again comes directly from French *agace* or *agasse*, which Cotgrave defined as "a pie, piannet, magatapie".

That the contents of pies were, to say the least, doubtful is clear from the sixteenth century proverb that "Pielid makes people wise", or as Lyly put it in 1592, "Pastry crust, eat enough and it will make you wise." The wisdom comes, explains Ray, from finding out what is inside, "because no man can tell what is in a pye till the lid be taken up."

Christmas pie seems to be so called because it was eaten at Christmas; it has no legends, no specific symbolism. Father Weisner does indeed maintain it "was born when Crusaders, returning from the Holy Land, brought along all sorts of Oriental spices. So it followed that the Lord's Nativity had to be celebrated with a pie containing spices from his native land." That these, however, were of merely minor importance can be seen from a recipe of 1394 which lists as essential

ingredients a pheasant, a hare, a capon, two partridges, two
pigeons and two rabbits, the livers and hearts of all these
animals, also two kidneys of sheep, little balls of beef, with
eggs and pickled mushrooms, as well as salt, pepper, vinegar
and various spices.

Even this was on the small side compared with some family
pies containing "butcher's meat, game, poultry and wild birds",
which weighed as much as a hundredweight and needed iron
bands to hold the pastry in place during baking. These gargan-
tuan dishes, first cut on Christmas Eve, provided a sort of
running buffet, cold slices being served to whoever might
happen to call.

Christmas pies nowadays are chiefly remembered because
of the impolite behaviour of one Master Horner. In the earliest
known version of this episode,

> Jack Horner, in the Corner,
> Eats good Christmas Pye,
> And with his Thumbs pulls out the Plumbs,
> And said, Good boy am I.

What does it mean? Anything? Some people believe it is good
history. Their theory, as given by the Opies, in the *Oxford Dictionary of Nursery Rhymes*, is that "the original Jack Horner was
steward to Richard Whiting, last of the abbots of Glastonbury.
. . . At the time of the Dissolution the abbot, hoping to appease
Henry VIII, sent his steward to London with a Christmas gift:
a pie in which were hidden the title deeds of twelve manors.
On the journey Jack Horner is said to have opened the pie
and extracted the deeds of the Manor of Mells in Somerset."

Though there is no proof either way, it is a fact that "one
Thomas Horner took up residence at Mells soon after the
Dissolution, and his descendants live there to this day." In
their defence, however, the Horner family point out that their
ancestor's name was Thomas, not Jack, that he "bought the

manor (together with several other manors and neighbouring farms)" for the sum of £1,831 9s 1¾d, and that the antiquary Leland confirms this, saying in 1543, "Mr. Horner hath bought the Lordship of the King."

On the other hand we know that Glastonbury, one of the richest foundations in the kingdom, was left untouched far longer than might be expected, and the State Papers themselves record that Abbot Whiting commonly sent Christmas gifts to the King. When at last he was brought to trial on the instructions of Thomas Cromwell, who had no doubt about the verdict, stating beforehand "the abbot of Glaston to be tried at Glaston, and also executed there with his complycys", one member of the jury that found him guilty is given as Thomas Horner. Nor does his name prove anything; anybody, say the Opies, "might be called Jack, particularly if he was believed to be a knave". Moreover in the sixteenth century "surprising things found their way into pies".

Among them perhaps the "four and twenty blackbirds" of another nursery rhyme. These also could be symbolic; two dozen not one dozen manorial deeds "baked in a pie" for the King who receives them, most appropriately, "in his counting house". Or, more poetically, the singing birds may represent "the choirs of dissolved monasteries making a dainty pie for Henry VIII". But in this case there is no need to theorise. An Italian cookery book of 1549 actually gives instructions how to "make pies so that the birds may be alive in them and flie out when it is cut up." The object of this exercise, it seems, was that the sudden flight of the birds might put out the candles, frighten the ladies, and so cause "a diverting Hurley-Burley amongst the Guests in the Dark".

Whatever may be the truth about Little Jack Horner, Thomas Love Peacock has described his story as "one of the most splendid examples on record of the admirable practical doctrine of 'taking care of number one'." People who like to concern themselves with what is strictly not their business are still said to "have a finger in the pie", and the good things of life, particularly those which come to us unexpectedly, are known as plums.

"The coffin of our Christmas Pies, in shape long," said Selden in 1689, "is in imitation of the crutch", that is the *crèche* or crib. Before the Reformation these pies were always oblong or square; as late as the nineteenth century Southey could write of "old bridges dangerously narrow, and angles in them like the corners of an English mince-pie, for the foot passengers to take shelter in." The pie thus became a representation of the manger in which Christ was laid, and sometimes a figure of the Child would be put in a slight hollow at the top. For this reason they were denounced by Puritans as "an abomination, idolatry, superstition and popish observance", and they were forbidden by law.

With the Restoration they came back, having meanwhile acquired the new title of "Superstitious pies, Minc'd or Christmas Pies, so Nick-nam'd by the Puritans or Precisions." Here too appears the name by which we know them—mince-pie or minced-pie, as it was originally spelt. And with more civilised times they grew smaller and round instead of oblong, until they became the little patties we call mince-pies today. "The learned Dr. Parr", headmaster and Latin scholar, continued, however, to insist in 1825, "Please to say Christmas-pie, not mince-pie; mince-pie is Puritanical."

It was of course the meat they contained that was minced, from Old French *mincier*, Latin *minutiare*, to chop up or make smaller (hence a man who minces takes small, affected steps). And besides the "beef tongues and chopped chicken" more familiar ingredients appear in the seventeenth century—"raisins, orange and lemon peelings, sugar and various spices". This curious mixture was probably eaten by Pepys when he dined with Sir William Penn on January 6, 1662, the anniversary of his wedding. Besides "a chine of beef and other good cheer" they had "eighteen mince-pies in a dish, the number of years Sir William hath been married." Somewhat earlier, celebrating the pay-off of a ship at Dartford and "very merry telling of tales", Pepys records how he heard "of one Damford, that, being a black man, did scald his beard with mince-pie, and it came up again all white in that place, and continued to his dying day."

Nowadays, though we fill our pies with mince-meat, which is merely a contraction of "minced meat", we leave out the meat, substituting a mixture of "currants, raisins, sugar, suet, apples, almonds, candied peel, etc. . . . chopped small." No wonder our language is the despair of the world!

That other English institution, Christmas plum pudding, also has a long history. A flaming dish, called *viande ardente*, was served at a Yuletide feast in 1417. But this was probably more like snapdragon than the original poding or puddyng, as it is variously spelt. The word appears in English, no one knows whence, in the thirteenth century, and meant at first something remarkably like a sausage. Such a pudding consisted of "the stomach or one of the entrails of a pig, sheep or other animal, stuffed with a mixture of minced meat, suet, oatmeal, seasoning, etc." In form it was long and round and still survives as the black and white puddings made in the north. Nashe therefore was quite correct when he remarked in 1592 that "everything hath an end and a pudding hath two." And a mother would tell a child, persistently demanding something, "You must eat another yard of pudding first," implying he must wait till he is older.

Although a French word *bodin* or *boudin* occurs at about the same time with a similar meaning, etymologists haven't been able to prove a relationship. Even if they did we don't know where *bodin* came from. Some connect it with Latin *botulus*, a sausage (hence bowel, because of its shape, and botulism, a kind of food poisoning). Others relate pudding to Old English *puduc*, a wen or a wart, thus something which swells or bulges. Skeat accepts this, saying "the older sense was doubtless bag, from a Teutonic base *pud-*, to swell out," and cites "poddy, round and stout in the belly". But the *OED* is "not at all certain the notion of swelling enters into the original sense", while for good measure Webster produces a Low German *puddik*, meaning sausage. "A pound of mysteries," sometimes says the man who wants sausages. There is a great deal of mystery in puddings as well.

Either from their appearance or their contents or both, puddings in the fifteenth century could stand for the entrails of animals and of men. Grose quotes "I'll let out your puddings," as a cant phrase for stabbing in the guts. And when Mistress Quickly says of Falstaff, "By my troth, he'll yield the crow a pudding one of these days; the king has killed his heart," she means he is like to die. Properly speaking, however, to yield the crow a pudding signified to be hanged on a gibbet and left to dangle till the crows came and pecked away the flesh.

There are other equally unpleasant associations. Erasmus, who for his time was remarkably sensitive to dirt, complained when he was in Cambridge of the foul-smelling streets and especially "a stinking butchery" in Slaughterhouse Lane, near the Guildhall. He suggested that "a man should have been hired for forty shillings in the year to keep the butchery and the rest of the town sweet by carrying out the puddings, guts and stinking blood." It is, however, unlikely that the Corporation took any action.

As for the delightful sounding Pudding Lane in London, where the Great Fire started, it should surely have the appetising scent of "an eating-house and a pastry-cook's next door to each other", yet it got its name, according to Stow, "because the butchers of Eastcheap have their scalding-house for hogs there, and their puddings, with other filth of beasts, are voided down that way to their Dung-boats on the Thames."

Some people rejoice (or otherwise) in the surname of Pudding. This was once, says Reaney, a common nickname for a round, stout, pot-bellied man; also perhaps for a butcher, "either from the sausages or puddings he sold or from the puddings or offal from his slaughter-house, a perpetual nuisance to his neighbours." As for Puddifoot or Puddephat, this is probably a combination of puddy or poddy and Old English *faet*, a vessel or vat. Its meaning is "round and stout vessel, cask, barrel", and so another nickname for "a man with a prominent paunch."

The early pudding, it seems clear, was first cousin to a haggis. An English writer in 1615 confirms this. "Small Oatmeal," he says "mixed with Blood and the Liver of either Sheep, Calfe or Swine, maketh that pudding which is called the Haggas or Haggus, of whose goodness it is vain to boast, because there is hardly to be found a man that doth not affect them." Haggises nowadays have all emigrated to Scotland; at one time however "hagas" or "habbys" was equally common in the south.

Some derive this word from the French *hachis*, which developed through the spellings *hache* and *hachy* into English hash, but except that haggis in Cumberland was called hash pudding, there seems no definite connexion. Another suggestion derives it from an old verb hag, to cut or chop, or the Anglo-Saxon *haecan*, to hack into pieces. Or again it may be related to the ancient name for a magpie, haggess. Whatever its origin and distressing though it may be to patriotic Scots, the word, like the dish, is definitely English. Haggis, says the *OED*, is "now considered especially Scotch, but (was) a popular dish in English cookery down to the beginning of the eighteenth century." The Gaelic *taigeis* is merely a transliteration of the English spelling.

"O what a glorious sight, warm-reekin', rich!" cries Burns, addressing the "great chieftain of the puddin'-race". And this was certainly no food for the cold table. "Puddings and paramours," advises a seventeenth century proverb, "should be hotly handled", which Kelly explains as meaning "Puddings, when cold, are uneatable, and love, when coldrife, is near the breaking off." Hence the complementary saying, "You must eat some cold pudding, to settle your love."

Pudding was formerly served "at the beginning of a meal . . . making the first dish". If a visitor arrived when the pudding was on the table, he stood a good chance of being invited to dine. In such a case, recorded Addison, "the ordinary Salutation is, Sir, I am glad to see you, you are come in Pudding-time." This last phrase became proverbial, pudding time being "the time when puddings are to be had, hence a time when one is in luck, a favorable or useful time."

According to nursery tradition Good King Arthur (or sometimes Stephen, Henry or Good Queen Bess) was fond of puddings. He went so far as to steal "three pecks of barley meal", and with this as a basis

> A bag pudding the king did make
> And stuffed it full of plums,
> And in it put great lumps of fat
> As big as my two thumbs.

His recipe sounds very like one given by Tryon in 1692: "In Puddens it is usual to mix Flour, Eggs, Milk, Raisins or Currants, and sometimes both Spice, Suet, the Fat or Marrow of Flesh, and several other things." Sweet puddings began to appear in the sixteenth century; instead of being cooked in the stomach of an animal they were boiled in a bag or a cloth, hence the name bag-pudding. This practice was widespread and quite probably still continues; Dickens noted "a smell like washing-day" in the Crachit household at Christmas, a most accurate description of a hot wet pudding cloth.

Soon puddings became so various both in composition and in the way they were cooked no definition could possibly cover them all. An ecstatic French visitor to England in the eighteenth century, however, had a most praiseworthy try: "The Pudding is a Dish very difficult to be describ'd, because of the several Sorts there are of it: Flower, Milk, Eggs, Butter, Sugar, Suet, Marrow from Bones, Raisins, etc., are the most common Ingredients of a Pudding. They bake them in an Oven, they boil them with Meat, they make them fifty several Ways. BLESSED BE HE THAT INVENTED PUDDING!" Nowadays, says the *OED* with typical English reserve, "its meaning and application are rather indefinite", or, as George Meredith scornfully remarked, "our English pudding (is) a fortuitous concourse of all the sweets in the grocer's shop."

Popular though pudding was, it did not become a recognised Christmas dish until the time of the Georges. Parson Woodforde on December 25, 1790, "dined . . . on rost Beef and Plumb Pudding". And in the nineteenth century Christmas plum pudding, "composed of flour, bread-crumbs, suet, raisins, currants and other fruits, with eggs, spice, etc., sometimes flavoured with brandy or other spirit", really came into its own. The mixing and boiling, usually in the copper where water was heated for the weekly wash, became a great ceremony. Every member of the family had to give a stir for luck, and the proper time for this was "the Sunday next before Advent", five weeks before Christmas and most appropriately known as Stir-up Sunday, from the Collect for the day which begins, "Stir up, we beseech thee, O Lord, the wills of thy faithful people."

So much for the pudding; what of the plums? A plum-pudding is or should be made of fresh plums. As one Taylor remarked in 1813, "Little Jack Horner, we fear, misapplies

the word plum, when he calls a dried raisin or currant by
that name. The bullace pudding, the prune pudding, and the
damascene pudding are better entitled to be called plum-
pudding than the currant or raisin puddings which have usurped
that appellation."

True enough. But early recipies all contain prunes, and at
first in the language there was no clear distinction between
fresh plums and dried prunes. The two words are basically
the same, coming from Greek *proumnon*, Latin *prunus*, both
meaning a plum-tree. Prune comes directly from Latin, the
Old English plume or ploume from the Greek, the change
from *r* to *l* being quite common. "In France and Spain,"
quoted a writer in 1633, "they drie their plummes . . . these
kinds we commonly call prunes." That is, we gave the dried
imported fruit an imported French name, *prunes*, just as grapes
when dried and imported are known by their French name,
raisins.

Then to complicate matters still further "the dried grapes
we term simply raisins when used for eating uncooked (we
call) plums when they form an ingredient in the famous
English plum pudding," or the famous English plum duff,
also known as Spotted Dick. This use, remarks the *OED*
learnedly, "probably arose from the substitution of raisins for
dried plums or prunes as an ingredient of plum-porridge, etc.,
with retention of the name plum for the substituted article."
In other words we just use raisins and call them plums; nor
does it strike us that there is anything odd about this proceeding.

Christmas pies and Christmas puddings have always been
very dear to English hearts. At the time of the Restoration
a jubilant writer proclaimed, "There is your Christmas pye
and that hath plums in abundance . . . He that discovered the
new star in Cassiopeia deserves not half so much to be remembered as he that first married meat and raisins together." And

contemplating the pudding, decorated with its sprig of holly and aflame with brandy, the *Illustrated London News* in 1848 became positively lyrical: "A kiss is round, the horizon is round, the earth is round, the sun and the stars, and all the host of heaven are round. So is plum pudding." In those days, of course, it was, being cooked tied up in a cloth. Now we use a foil-covered basin or get it out of a tin. The glory has indeed departed; Dickens wouldn't like it at all.

6

CAROUSING AND HEALTH-DRINKING

Words are born, they change and develop, often they die. Sometimes, however, they survive like fossils, isolated in a special context, not dead yet not alive. Wassail is such a word. Every Christmas we cheerfully sing:

> Love and joy come to you,
> And to you your wassail too,
> And God bless you, and send you
> A happy new year.

But apart from its having something to do with drink, wassail for most people is almost meaningless.

Yet once it was a common, ordinary, polite form of greeting or leave taking. "Freond saeithe to freonde," wrote Layamon in 1205, "Leofue freond, was hail", that is, Dear friend, be well, be of good health, be fortunate, live long. The phrase is very old and seems to have come to us from the Danes or the Vikings. Warriors in *Beowulf* call to each other when they meet, *Waes thu hal*.

These simple familiar words occur with great poignancy in Anglo-Saxon translations of the Bible. "Hail to thee, King of the Jews," cry the Roman soldiers, mocking Christ—*Hal wes thu, Judea cyning*. In exactly the same way the angel greets Mary—*Hal wes thu, Maria*. And after the Resurrection Christ says to his disciples, *Avete*, all hail, or *Hale wese ye*. Our nearest modern phrase is of course farewell, interpreted as "proceed happily" and properly addressed to one about to start on a

E   59

⬤

journey. But even this has long been regarded as literary or even archaic.

The word hail itself is in a state of extraordinary confusion. It began as *heill*, meaning whole, in good health, and also good luck. In Anglo-Saxon it became *hal* or *hale*; with the sense of "in good health" it survives, again fossilised, in the phrase "hale and hearty". It is the same word as whole, but as a greeting it developed into hail. "Hayl thow, mary" is the medieval version of *Ave, Maria*, and "Hail, Mary" the prayer remains in English to this day, though a modern translation attempts to substitute "Greetings!"

Shakespeare's witches used the old construction: "All hail, Macbeth! Hail to thee, Thane of Cawdor." Now, except for being "Hail-fellow-well-met" or "on easy familiar terms" with someone, we have abandoned this gracious greeting for the ugly, vulgar and meaningless Hullo! Yet men and ships still sometimes hail each other, and police use loud-hailers to make their voices heard.

There are other, more sinister connexions. When Germany had a king, "Long live the King!" was *Heil dem Könige!* When Germany had a dictator the cry changed to *Heil, Hitler*, and this with the heels clicked and the right hand raised in ancient Roman fashion became the famous Nazi salute. The "frozen vapour falling in pellets", however, is no relation; this kind of hail comes from Old English *haegl*, related to Greek *kakhlex*, a pebble.

The association of wassail with drinking is very early. In Anglo-Saxon times a host offering his guest a cup would wish him *Was hail*. Whereupon, if he knew his manners, the guest would reply *Drinc hail*. This latter phrase, says Skeat, "is almost untranslatable, meaning literally 'drink, hale', i.e. drink and good luck be with you", but the polite intention is clear enough. There are several references to this odd habit of the English in the twelfth and thirteenth centuries, usually remarked on by their Norman conquerors. According to Robert de Brunne,

> This is ther custom and hev gest
> When they are at the ale or fest:
> Ilk man that levis gware him drink
> Salle say Wosseille to him drink;
> He that biddis sall say Wassaile,
> The tother salle say again, Drinkaille.

How this custom arose is not known, though the twelfth century chronicler Geoffrey of Monmouth traced it back to the Jutes. His tale is that about the year 450 Hengist and his brother Horsa came from Jutland to Kent, either because they had been exiled or because Vortigern, the king of South Britain, had asked for their help against invaders, or for both reasons. They were kindly received and given land in the Isle of Thanet. Soon, finding the life a good one, Hengist sent for his daughter Rowena. He then invited Vortigern to a feast, in the course of which "Ronewenne . . . come with a coupe of golde and knelede before the king, and saide to him, Whatsaile!" Not knowing how to answer, the king inquired what he should say and was told, "Drink hail, so Drinkhayle, quoth this kyng agen, and bed hire drink anon . . . That was the first time that whatsaile and drynkehaile come up into this lande; and from that time unto this time it hath been wel usede." Meanwhile Vortigern had fallen violently in love, married Rowena, and gave her father in return the whole Kingdom of Kent.

Sad to say, no one now believes this charming story. But certainly by the time of the Norman Conquest the English had already acquired a reputation for drinking deep and Geoffrey spoke no lie when he said the custom he described "hath been wel usede". In 1190 Nigellus Wireker, writing of the English students at the University of Paris, praised

them "for generosity and other virtues", but also remarked
that they were "too much addicted to wessail and dringail".
And Wace of Jersey, in his history of the Dukes of Normandy,
describes with great vividness the night before the Battle of
Hastings. "When it was time to fight the battle", he says in
Skeat's translation, "on the previous night, as I hear men
tell, the English were extremely hilarious, very full of laughter
and very cheerful. The whole night they ate and drank; never
throughout the night did they lie in bed. You might have seen
them stir about, skip, dance and sing."

Moreover the words they shouted were very strange to
Norman ears:

> *Bublie* crient e *weissel*
> E *laticome* e *drinckeheil,*
> *Drinc hindrewart* e *drintome*
> *Drinc helf* e *drinc tome.*

They are strange to us too, but Skeat explains them all. *Bublie*
is *beoth blithe,* be merry; *weissel* we know; *laticome* is *laet hine
cuman,* let him come; *drinc hindrewart* is drink towards me,
drink hitherward, *drintome* is drink to me and *drinc helf* is drink
half. Coming out of the night they must have been terrifying.
One wonders if the English were over-confident or merely
keeping up their spirits. It hardly seems surprising that they
lost the battle.

By the fourteenth century wassail had almost lost its original
form and become both a verb, meaning "to sit carousing and
health-drinking", and a noun, meaning "riotous festivity and
revelling" and also "the liquor in which healths were drunk".
Yet though Claudius in *Hamlet* is said nightly to "keep
wassail", and Antony who, in Egypt with Cleopatra, "fishes,
drinks and wastes The lamps of night in revel", is urged to
"leave thy lasicious wassails", the word soon acquired a specific
rather than a general association. "Wassail", explained Phillips

in 1658, "an ancient ceremonious custom, still used upon twelf day at night, of going about with a great bowl of Ale, drinking of healths."

This manner of drinking, with the cup going round the table, was also an English practice. "It was their custom", says Brand, "at all their feasts, for the master of the house to fill a large bowl or pitcher, and drink out of it first himself, and then give it to him that sat next, and so it went around." This is the cup which later in monasteries and universities "received the honourable appellation of *Poculum Caritatis* or loving cup." But when it appeared, as it always did, at Christmas or Twelfth Night, it was known as the Wassail bowl, "a browne bowle, drest with Ribbands" and filled with a liquor "made of honied wine or sweet mead, with hearbes in it". A book of Household Ordinances of the fourteenth century shows with what ceremony it was brought in: "When the steward cometh in at the hall door with the wassell, he must crie three time, Wassell, wassell, wassell, and then the chapell (chaplain) is to answer with a songe."

Meanwhile the wassail-bowl went out from the hall to the streets. Every festival seems to have been seized on by the poor as an excuse for demanding money, and an eighteenth century writer tells us " 'twas an ancient custom amongst the poor people to go a-wesseling at Christmas . . . Such poor people went about to get money to drink your health, and for which they carried a box to put their money in." From this, 'wesseling' came also to be "a name given to the singing of Christmas carols at the doors of houses". That they were not always appreciated we know from Beaumont and Fletcher, for one of their characters remarks, "Have you done your wassayl? 'tis a handsome drousie dittie I'll assure ye, now I had as leave hear a Cat cry."

But the box or bowl wasn't always empty. At one time, according to Brand, "Young Women went about with a

Wassail-bowl, that is a Bowl of spiced Ale, on New Year's
Eve." Passers-by were still asked for money and received in
return a drink. This practice became so common Selden uses it
in 1654 to emphasise his anti-Romanism, for, he says, "the
Pope in sending Rellicks to Princes, does as Wenches do by their
Wassels at New-Year's-tide, they present you with a cup and
you must drink of the slabby stuff; but the meaning is, you
must give them Moneys, ten times more than it is worth."
Pepys also noted the custom, though his spelling is all his
own. "We went into an alehouse and there eat some cakes
and ale, and a washeall-bowl woman and girle came to us and
sung to us." Unfortunately he doesn't mention what happened
next.

Other wassailers, "such as in the country go about from
House to House during the festival of Christmas, and sing
Catches for Drink and other small Boon," presented their
empty bowl to be filled with ale or beer. As the old carol
says:

> Come, butler, come fill us a bowl of the best,
> Then we hope that your soul in heaven may rest;
> But if you do draw us a bowl of the small,
> Then down shall go butler, bowl and all.

An old man in Herefordshire remembered well in 1912 how
"when I was a boy we used to go a-wassailing. We had a
punchbowl or wassail bowl. It was a big one made of beech-
wood and would hold about two gallons. They took it round
at night, decorated with ribbons and coloured streamers.
Beginning some little time before Christmas, they visited all
the houses of the neighbourhood. They sang songs and
carols. At each house the bowl was filled with punch,
made of hot cider, gin, nutmeg and sugar. They had toast
with it and money was also given." Luckily no one in those

days was likely to be run in for drunken driving on the way home.

What is surely the oddest development of this custom comes from the north of England and was observed until quite recently. Here the wassail or wessel-bowl has been transformed through coincidence of sound into a Vessel-cup. Yet this was neither a vessel nor a cup nor had it any connexion with wassailing or with drink. Instead it was something much more unexpectedly Popish, a box containing "two dolls dressed up to represent the Virgin and the infant Christ, decorated with ribbons and surrounded by flowers and apples." The more elaborate versions had a glass lid, others were simply covered by a clean white napkin or a cloth. It was "carried from door to door on the arms of a woman who . . . on reaching a house, uncovered the box and sang." A convenient superstition provided that "to send her away without giving her a donation is considered unlucky". Sometimes these Vessel-cups were known as "the Doll-in-a-box", or as Milly boxes, a contraction of My Lady boxes.

Meanwhile in the south of England wassailing had developed into a kind of fertility rite. "At Twelve-tyde at night", quoted Aubrey in 1686, "they use in the Countrey to wassaile their Oxen and to have Wassaile-Cakes made." Though it was indeed the custom to drink to, or worsle as they called it in Sussex, "in order to ensure their thriving", the cattle and even the beehives, the more usual recipients of this attention were fruit-trees, especially cider apples. The time for this nocturnal sallying-forth varied from Christmas Eve to Old Twelfth Night, but the procedure was always basically the same. The farmer, his family and workmen assembled in the kitchen, collected a jar, a bottle or a bowl of cider and set out for the orchards. Sometimes a gun was fired, possibly with the idea of scaring off evil spirits. Everyone joined in the wassailing proper, which consisted of "throwing some of the cider about the roots

of the trees and then, forming themselves into a ring, singing
a song:

> Health to thee, good apple tree,
> Well to bear, pocket fulls, hat fulls,
> Peck fulls, bushel-bag fulls.''

Whereupon no doubt, they all went home and made merry on
the rest of the cider.

Incidentally the wassail-cakes, which Aubrey mentions, and
the wassail-bread of which we sometimes hear, are misnomers.
Their appearance is due to a confusion with wastell-bread.
Wastel or guastel, the same word as modern French *gâteau*,
meant bread made of finest flour, white and refined instead of
coarse-ground, and therefore much more expensive. This
bread was likely to be provided at a high feast such as Christmas,
and quite naturally attracted to itself the name of Wassail cake.
The man who made or sold these wastels was known as a
wasteler or wastelmonger, hence such surnames as Wastell,
Wassall or Wassell.

Bread or rather toast was, however, often associated with
the wassail-bowl, and commonly found floating in it. Putting
toasted bread in our drinks seems to have been an ancient
English habit; Falstaff orders, "Go fetch me a quart of sack;
put a toast in't." From this comes the equally English custom
of "proposing a toast" when we wish to drink the health of
some person or good cause.

Whether Steele's story of its origin, given by him in *The
Tatler* in 1709, is true or not, it is certainly worth repeating.
"Many wits of the last age", he says, "will assert that the
word, in its present sense, was known amongst them in their
youth, and had its rise from an accident at the town of Bath,
in the reign of Charles the Second. It happened that, on a
public day, a celebrated beauty of the times was in the Cross
Bath, and one of the crowd of her admirers took a glass of the
water in which the fair one stood, and drank her health to

the company. There was in the place a gay fellow, half fuddled, who offered to jump in, and swore, though he liked not the liquor, he would have the toast. He was opposed in his resolution; yet this Whim gave foundation to the present honour which is done to the lady we mention in our liquors, who has ever since been called a toast."

The actual contents of the wassail-bowl seem to have varied extensively over the centuries. As the custom is Saxon in origin the basic component of the drink was usually ale, that is malt liquor made without hops. To this was added, says Brand, "nutmeg, sugar, toast and roasted crabs or apples." Winter, according to Shakespeare, is the time "when roasted crabs hiss in the bowl", perhaps that gossip's bowl where Puck would sometimes lurk

> In very likeness of a roasted crab;
> And, when she drinks, against her lips I bob
> And on her withered dewlap pour the ale.

This is the drink that appeared so enticingly on Christmas Eve at Dingley Dell, "a mighty bowl of wassail, something smaller than an ordinary wash-house copper, in which the hot apples were hissing and bubbling with a rich look and a jolly sound that were perfectly irresistible."

The name of this concoction was Lamb's Wool, "a drink consisting of hot ale mixed with the pulp of roasted apples, and sugared and spiced", very popular from the sixteenth century, a great favourite of Pepys and also of the poet Robert Herrick:

> Next crowne the bowle full
> With gentle lamb's-wooll;
> Adde sugar, nutmeg and ginger;
> With store of ale too;
> And thus ye must doe
> To make the Wassaile a swinger.

In a contemporary receipt "the pulpe of the roasted apples, in number foure or five, is mixed in a wine quart of faire water, laboured together until it come to be as apples, and ale, which we call lambes wool." The name, it is clear, derives from the white frothy pulp of the apples, looking like sheared wool. This whiteness may also account for the reference to "blanket" which occurs in a description of Henry VIII's Twelfth Night feast at Richmond in 1516: "Then was the wassail or blanket brought in, and so brake up Christmasse." For blanket, from French *blanc*, meant originally "white woollen stuff".

By the nineteenth century hot cider is substituted for ale, and even gin. And in Cumberland we have a record of a wassail cup "introduced long before visitors separate; its contents include old Jamaica rum, hot water, sugar and lemon". Here however there seems to have been a crossing of traditions, for this is Punch and quite another thing.

7

THE THREE KINGS AND KING BEAN

The feast "that men clepeth the Epyphany" has never been much celebrated in this country. It belongs to the Church Calendar, not to popular speech, and perhaps for this reason, though we borrowed the word through French *epiphanie*, it remains almost unchanged from late Latin *epiphania* and even Greek *epiphaneia*. This is usually defined as appearance, manifestation; from the verb *epiphainein*, a compound of *epi*, to, upon, and *phainein*, to show. It is related to *phantos*, visible, yet seems to carry the sense of being misty, luminous, transparent, all of which are exemplified in phantom, our name for a ghost.

An epiphany, then, is a manifestation or a striking appearance. According to one definition it was "originally used of the visit paid by a king to his subjects, when he would appear before them in magnificence and splendour to receive their homage." More usually it was applied to "a manifestation or appearance of some divine or super-human being", in which sense it was adopted by the Church to describe "the advent or 'appearing' of Christ". Moreover it seems to have acquired a double significance, relating both to the incarnation of Christ, the word made flesh, and also the showing forth or revelation of his more than human powers.

In its early centuries the Church celebrated only three great festivals—Easter, Pentecost, and "the feast of the Lord's Epiphany", held, for what reason is not exactly clear, on January 6. This day commemorated the start of Christ's ministry with his baptism in the Jordan, when "a voice came from heaven, which said, Thou art my beloved Son; in thee I am well pleased." For, as Saint John Chrysostom explained, preaching in Antioch in 386, "we give the name Epiphany to the day of our Lord's baptism because he was not made manifest to all when he was born, but only when he was baptized, for until that time he was unknown to the people at large." This is confirmed by Saint Jerome, who says that the idea of "showing forth" belonged not to his birth in the flesh, for then "he was hidden and not revealed", but rather to the baptism in Jordan, "when the heavens were opened upon Christ".

Since the feast was "a celebration of all manifestations of the divine nature of Christ", it gathered to itself other events and occasions by which he revealed "what he is and what he does". Among these were the finding of the Child by his parents disputing with the Doctors in the Temple, the feeding of the five thousand, and more especially the changing of the water into wine at the marriage feast at Cana, "God manifesting himself by miracle in human nature", as Saint Augustine saw it.

Epiphany or *Hemera ton Photon*, the Day of Light, was kept with considerable solemnity in the Eastern Church. In the West, by the fourth century, Christmas was the great occasion and Epiphany little regarded. About this time, however, the two did a sort of swop; Christmas was adopted by the East and Epiphany in turn by the West, both feasts from then on being observed by both Churches.

For the Romans Epiphany had quite a different emphasis, being solemnised principally, as Butler says, "in honour of the revelation Jesus Christ made of himself to the Magi, or wise men; who soon after his birth . . . came to worship him and give him presents." These sages, whatever their race or occupation, were certainly not Jews; that they should have been summoned so early and by such a spectacular sign as a star in heaven was taken as a clear indication that the Son of Man had been sent to the Gentiles as well as to the Chosen People.

Magus was the title given to the ancient Persian scholar-priests, skilled in oriental magic and astrology, readers of omens and interpreters of dreams. Who these particular wise men might be we are not told, nor how many of them came, though "the general opinion", as Butler somewhat cautiously remarks, "opts for three". But tradition, that inexhaustible mine of unreliable information, knows all about the Magi. They were eastern kings riding great camels who brought princely presents of frankincense, gold and myrrh:

Tres Reges Regi Regum tria dona ferebant,
Myrrhum Homini, Uncto Aurum, Thura dedere Deo.

Their names were Caspar, Melchior and Balthazar, and it was generally assumed that one of them was black. In due course, so the story goes, they were baptized by Saint Thomas, the Apostle of the East, and later martyred.

For some reason all of them were buried at Constantinople, "whence the Empress Helena caused them to be transported to Milan by an Italian, from whom a noble family at Florence obtained the surname of Epiphania". This sounds, to say the least, unlikely, though it can't be denied that the Florentine Telephone Directory still includes subscribers called Epifani, Epifanio and Epifania. Sad to say, they are probably so called because one of their ancestors was born on January 6.

As for the Three Kings, they were not even now at rest, for the conquering Frederick Barbarossa stole their relics and took them to Cologne. Here, by common consent, they remain and the Germans at one time were very proud of their acquisition. Epiphany with them is *Dreikönistag* or *Dreikönigsfest*, just as in France it is known as *Le Jour des Rois*. It would be pleasant to believe that the charmingly named village of Threekingham in Lincolnshire had some connexion with these eastern sages. If so it was merely in the minds of romantic country people, adapting it from its original form of Threckingham, the home of the tribe of Threc.

In Italy Epiphany has been transformed into a little old woman dressed in black, known as *La Strega*, the witch (also the name of a well known liqueur), as *La Vecchia*, the old woman, or most commonly as Santa Befana, a simple corruption of the title of the feast. Befana is the Italian Father Christmas, "an ugly but good-natured old hag who leaves presents in the stockings of children on the Eve of the Epiphany . . . giving to the good," says the American *Dictionary of Folklore*, "candy and sweetmeats; stones and charcoal are left for the naughty ones." The children, of course, do their best to stay awake, and cry out, *Ecco la Befana!* when the little old lady appears.

She too has her legend; indeed she has more than one. Some say the Magi, Gaspare, Melchiore and Baldassare, were her three sons. But the commonest story tells how she was invited by these same Wise Men to go with them to worship the Christ Child and to offer their gifts. She refused, complaining she was much too busy cleaning her house. She would, she said, wait for their return, when she could hear all about their trip. She never saw them again for they went back by another way. So on the Eve of every Epiphany she watches in case they pass. Or according to another version, after the Magi had gone she changed her mind, set off to follow them but lost herself and never arrived at Bethlehem. Even now she is still searching for the Baby, looking in all the houses where there are children and leaving behind the presents he should have had.

In earlier times La Befana played a more sinister rôle, symbolising the approach of Lent and the beginning of the penitential season. This Befana was "a frightful black doll, with an orange at her feet, and seven skewers thrust through her, one of which is pulled out at the end of each week in Lent." Such rag-doll effigies were hung outside the doors of houses or displayed in windows as "a token that those who exhibit her mean to observe a rigorous fast." Moreover it used to be the custom, and maybe still is, for young and old in Rome and many other cities and towns to "assemble and make a great noise in her honor with trumpets, tambourines, drums and tin-horns", and for singers and musicians to serenade her ugly figure.

In this guise, half hated, half loved, she has quite a different story. Some say the black doll represents Herodias, mother of Salome, repenting perhaps of her impulsive demand for John the Baptist's head upon a charger. But the tale they tell in Florence is that "Befana was the Christian name of a damsel of the Epifania family before-mentioned; that she offended the fairies and was by them tempted to eat a sausage in Lent, for which transgression she was sawn asunder in the Piazza, and has ever since been hung in effigy at the end of the Carnival, as a warning to all beholders." Fasting regulations were taken a little more seriously then than they are today.

In the Greek Church Epiphany was sometimes called *Theophania*. From *phainein* and *theos*, a god, this means specifically "the manifestation or appearance of God or a god to man". We never used it here, but in France it was at one time quite common, most charmingly corrupted to *Tiphanie*, *Tifinie* or *Tifaigne*, to name three of the forty or so different spellings known. It found its way into English as Tiffany, but as a name for the feast it won no popular acceptance. Almost its only appearances are in legal or court documents, generally written in French; in Edward II's Household Ordinances there is an entry for *Le Jour de la Tyffaine*.

Yet the word was known, for by the sixteenth century it had developed a sense peculiar to English, that of "a kind of thin transparent silk, also a transparent gauze, muslin, cobweb lawn". One authority relates it not to Epiphany but to a French verb *tifer*, to dress silk, but Littré makes no mention of this verb. The *OED* says "it is usually taken to be short for Epiphany silk", to which Brewer gratuitously adds that "the

F

material was so called because it used to be worn at the Epiphany revels". This explanation would be stronger if any record existed of the phrase "Epiphany silk"; none has been found.

Indeed the *OED*'s second suggestion seems more probable, that "it was a fanciful name, with allusion to the sense 'manifestation' "—though perhaps "revelation" conveys better the impression intended. For tiffany silk was the original "see-through" fabric—when a woman wore it you could see the woman, provided that was all she wore. So Holland noted in 1601 "the invention of that fine silk, Tiffanie, Sarcenet, and Cypres, which instead of apparell to cover and hide, shew women naked through them". And somewhat later John Evelyn, touring Italy, wrote of Venetian ladies "shewing their naked arme, through false sleeves of Tiffany, girt with a bracelet or two."

Not all tiffany was so luscious. It had its place in the kitchen, being "a plain-weave open mesh cotton fabric, such as cheese-cloth", or a "strong, fine-meshed gauze out of which sieves are made". Such a sieve, especially in the north of England, was also known as a tiffany, while tempting-sounding tiffany cakes were so called because they were made of "wheaten flour, which was separated from the bran by being worked through a hair sieve or tiffany".

A tiffany could even be a garment, provided it was thin and transparent, or a head-dress:

> A tiffany shee wore about her head,
> Hanginge submissely to her shoulders white.

As an adjective it meant delicate, flimsy, fragile; Webster's example, "a tiffany-winged fly", is a delightful description. And there was the dramatist who wrote in 1658 of "a tiffany plot; any man with half an eye may easily see through it." Our language is the poorer for losing this expressive word, which lingers, if at all, only as a most unusual given name.

For though we occasionally had our Theophanias and our Epiphanias, a girl born on January 6 was more likely to be called Tiffany. The name appears in England during the twelfth century, introduced, as so often, from France:

> William de Coningsby
> Came out of Brittany,
> With his wife Tiffany,
> And his maid Manfras,
> And his dog Hardigras.

Though it survived longer in Cornwall, it mostly became unpopular with other 'popish' names at the time of the Reformation, and virtually disappeared. A male version, Tiphina, occurs in 1322, but this is extremely rare. So is the corresponding Epiphanius, though there exists in Bath Abbey a tomb carved by Epiphanius Evesham, round about 1643.

Rather surprisingly Tiffany, sometimes shortened to Tiffen or Tiffin, is also a surname, far better known in America than it is here. For it was Charles Lewis Tiffany who opened in New York in 1837 the "small stationery and notion store on a thousand dollars capital" loaned by his father that later grew into one of the most famous jewel houses in the world, numbering among its customers more than twenty-four emperors and kings. And Charles Lewis gave his name Tiffany to a kind of jewel setting, "having long prongs to hold a gem".

In England only the learned spoke of Epiphany. Commonly the season was called Twelvetide or Twelftide, and the feast itself, January 6, Twelfth Day. This dates back to the time of King Alfred, who is said to have promulgated "a Law . . . with relation to holidays, by virtue of which the twelve days

after the Nativity of our Saviour were made festivals"—the
twelve days of Christmas, as they were later known. Nor did
the people need urging to be gay; in medieval courts and
great houses feasting and celebration continued undiminished till the final revel of Twelfth Night. Nowadays
the superstitious among us mark Twelfth Day merely by
taking down our Christmas decorations, if we haven't already
burned them because they harboured the dust.

Twelfth Night, of course, precedes Twelfth Day. There is
increasing confusion over this because we have long forgotten
the ancient custom of starting the day not at midnight but at
six the previous evening. We do know Christmas Eve comes
before Christmas Day, but forget that this is also Christmas
Night. So the last great festival of Christmas—eating, drinking,
dancing, mumming, foolery and plays—was actually held on
what to us would be the night of January 5 to 6. *Twelfth Night,
or What You Will*, typical of Shakespeare's lack of interest in
titles, was almost certainly written for one of these entertainments.

"This is the Even of the Three Kings of Collen", wrote a
priest of Louvain in 1569, "at which all good Catholics make
merry and crie, 'The King Drinks'." This king was not one
of the Magi or even of royal blood; he was *Le Roi de la Fève* or
King Bean, ruler only for a night:

> Thir Kyngs thai ar bot kyngs of bane,
> And schort wyl heir thare tyme be gane.

For the *pièce de résistance* of this feast was the Twelfth Night
Cake or *Gâteau de la Fève*, a large flat cake made of flour, sugar,
honey, ginger, pepper and probably dried fruit; one recipe
moreover mentions eighteen eggs. Like our Christmas cakes it
was frosted or iced, and usually decorated. Hidden in it some-
where were a pea and a bean. The cake was carefully divided
and everyone given a slice. Whoever found the bean in his

portion, either by accident or by clever contrivance, was King for the evening; whoever found the pea was his Queen.

> Now, now the mirth comes
> With the cake full of plums,
> Where Beane's the King of the Sport here;
> Besides, we must know
> The Pea also
> Must revell, as Queene, in the Court here.

Once appointed, the King's traditional cry was:

> *Grâce à la fève, je suis roi;*
> *Nous le voulons, versez à boire!*

And once he had drained his glass the whole company followed him, shouting aloud, "The King drinks!" This procedure was repeated so often during the evening that a story current in London in the sixteenth century tells of a curate "who having taken his preparations over evening, when all men say (as the manner is), the King drinketh, chanting his Masse the next morning, fell asleep in his memento"—where the priest made a pause to remember the names of those he has been asked to pray for—"and when he awoke, added with a loud voice, the King drinketh."

Yet when the wine was all drunk and the revelry done and the merry company dispersed, the King had the privilege or rather the melancholy duty of footing the bill—poor King Bean "whom after they have honoured with drinking his health, and shouting aloud, *Le Roy boit*, they make pay for all the reckoning."

Even so these kings for a night must have thought the game worth the candle, for they passed into a proverb. "He has found the bean in the cake", says Brewer, meaning "he has got a prize in the lottery, has come to some unexpected good fortune." The *OED* has a different version, "Boast that you have found the bean in the cake"; this goes right back to Montaigne, who wrote in 1580, *Vantez vous d'avoir trouvé la febre au gasteau*, which the *OED* interprets as "a reference to appointing as King of the company on Twelfth-night the man in whose portion of cake the bean was found. Afterwards proverbial for hitting the mark or being lucky." Our other references to beans are, however, unrelated; even a bean-feast has no connexion with Twelfth Night.

There were once many other Twelvetide customs; they are mostly pagan and have left no mark on the language. Among them was the lighting of fires, and the most spectacular fire of them all is the Viking ship that goes up in flames in Shetland at Up-helly-a. This apparently outlandish word turns out to be no more than a variant of the old Scottish name for Twelfth Day—Uphaliday, the day "on which the Holy or holidays are supposed to be 'up' ", in the sense of being completed, ended —"It's all up with him", as we sometimes say. From this came Uphalimass for the feast of Epiphany, Uphelly Even and Uphelya or Up-helly-a, where, says the *OED*, "the final -a may stand for *all*", an explanation which scarcely explains.

Not content with Uphaliday, the Scots used at one time to celebrate on January 18 what was known as Old Twelfth Day or sometimes Four an' Twenty Day. This confusion about dates which from the middle of the eighteenth century affected all our fixed feasts was due to the change in the calendar in 1752. For to bring ourselves into line with the rest of Europe we then adopted the Gregorian or New Style of reckoning, and had to advance our dates by eleven days. Thus by Act of Parliament September 2 that year was followed by September 14, which led to rioting and protests in the London streets, the slogan being, "Give us back our eleven days!"

The strangest result of this change was that Christmas Day then fell on the date that should have been Epiphany, to many people's lasting distress. For the radicals or New Stylers kept Christmas on what, to the diehards or Old Stylers, celebrating eleven days later, was only December 13. In the remoter districts, especially Scotland and the north, this bitter argument continued long unresolved. So January 6 was often referred to as Old Christmas Day and January 18 as Old Twelfth Day.

A contributor to *Notes and Queries* recorded as recently as 1859 that "the late Davie Gilbert used to tell of his own knowledge, how an old gentleman and lady always walked to Church in full dress, on the abandoned Christmas Day, and after vainly trying to enter, walked back and read the service at home." The Anglican Church, it would seem, had no service for Epiphany; moreover, unless the vicar kept them out, the building was apparently locked. Yet though they make a gallant couple it was just this kind of persistence that probably helped to kill the observance of Twelfth Night.

8

ONLY IN THE CARNIVAL

'Tis known, at least it should be, that throughout
All countries of the Catholic persuasion,
Some weeks before Shrove Tuesday comes about,
The people take their fill of recreation . . .
With fiddling, feasting, dancing, drinking, masking,
And other things which may be had for asking . . .
This feast is named the Carnival, which being
Interpreted, implies "farewell to flesh":
So call'd, because the name and thing agreeing,
Through Lent they live on fish, both salt and fresh.

Thus Byron who, when asked for his impressions of Italy and the Italians, remarked that "their best things are the Carnival balls and masquerades, where everybody runs mad for six weeks." They then for the rest of the year became exceeding sober, as Thomas Gray discovered when he visited Turin in November 1739.

Looking for entertainment, he was told, "There is an excellent Opera, but it is only in the Carnival: Balls every night, but only in the Carnival: Masquerades too, but only in the Carnival. This Carnival lasts only from Christmas to Lent: one half of the remaining part of the year is passed in remembering the last, the other in expecting the future Carnival. We cannot well subsist upon such slender diet."

How did it come about, this almost essentially Latin festivity which never as such found its way to England? The *Dictionary of Folklore* defines it as "a boisterous communal celebration dating back to the Middle Ages, and still observed

83

in most of Europe and the Americas. It features masquerades,
floats, torch processions, dances, fireworks, noise-making and
tomfoolery, which often reaches a point of nuisance and licen-
tiousness." And according to the proverb, "After a carnival
Lent ever follows", or, as Selden put it, "What the Church
debars us one day she gives us leave to take out in another—
first there is a Carnival and then a Lent."

It has been said that "in the Romish Church there was
antiently a feast immediately preceding Lent, which lasted
many days, called *Carniscapium*", here to be understood as
taking or eating of meat. But this seems to be neither true
nor likely, for the Church "never encouraged the riotous living
and the revelry of the Carnival . . . the priests recommended
their hearers to prepare themselves for Lent by abstinence from
pleasures."

Bishop Hall in the seventeenth century confirms this, re-
marking that priests and religious were not officially expected
to approve of such goings-on. It was their own parishioners
who often assured them the whole mad affair was entirely for
the good of their souls: "Howsoever it was by some sullen
authority forbidden to clerks and votaries of any kind to go
masked and misguised in those seemingly abusive solemnities,
yet more favourable construction hath offered to make them
believe that it was chiefly for their sakes, for the refreshment
of their sadder and more restrained spirits, that this free and
lawless Festivity was taken up."

The essence of Carnival has always been "Let us eat, drink
and be merry", the urgent need to make the most of the good
things of life for fear they may be taken away—"Men eat and
drink and abandon themselves to every kind of sportive foolery,
as if resolved to have their fill of pleasure before they were to
die, and as it were forego every sort of delight." And this
attitude has certainly led to some of the more fanciful deriva-
tions of the name of the season.

Carnival or, to give its Italian form, *carnevale*, seems originally to have applied to "the day preceding the first of Lent", that is Shrove Tuesday. Because it came before the fast many people shared Byron's idea that the word "being interpreted, implies 'farewell to flesh'." But this, says Skeat, was "promoted by a popular etymology which resolved the word into *carne*, flesh, and *vale*, farewell, as if the sense were, 'farewell, O flesh'." Others, adopting the French spelling *carnaval*, connect it with *aval*, as in avalanche, from *avaler*, to descend, thus meaning, "Down with flesh". There is even a suggestion that it may derive "from *carrus navalis*, cart of the sea, a boat-shaped vehicle on wheels used in the procession of Dionysus, and from which satirical songs were sung." In Florence and other cities cars were certainly drawn through the streets and satirical songs sung from them; people even got drunk, but this does not necessarily mean they were followers of Dionysus.

Indeed the name, if not the feast, most probably comes from Church Latin. Early documents mention the time of *carnelevarium*, *carnilevamen* or *carnelvale*, and these are clearly forms of *carnem levare*, "the putting away or removal of flesh (as food)". But even here there is still confusion, for *levare* could also have the sense of "to relieve, to ease", so that *carnelevarium* is taken as "the solace of the flesh (i.e. the body) before the austerities of Lent". Thus, says Skeat, "the word was often completely misunderstood and misapplied, and the sense was altered from 'a time of fasting' to 'a time of feasting'."

An exactly parallel phrase, from an eleventh century charter, is *carnem laxare*, "leaving or forsaking flesh". This became in Italian *carne lasciare*, then *carnesciale*, meaning, "apparently by contradiction" as the OED says, the "revelry and riotous amusement" that characterised the Carnival. A great feature of the festival in Florence was the singing of ribald verses known as *canti carnascialeschi*. Some of the city's most eminent writers, poets and philosophers delighted to compose them, and Lorenzo de Medici himself is said to have "raised these obscene songs . . . into an art".

Even here the contradiction over the name of the season does not end, for at one time Shrove Tuesday was known as *carnivora dies*, flesh eating day, or *carniscapium*, the taking of flesh; so in France they call it Fat Tuesday or *mardi gras*. Clearly everything depends upon whether the emphasis is put on the eating of meat before it is forbidden or the actual forbidding itself. Chance suggests this confusion arose because at one time even before Lent pleasures of every kind were abandoned by the devout, while their more worldly contemporaries were pampering the flesh: "thus the Carnival, while it meant feasting and revelry to the great majority, probably meant fasting or abstinence and reclusion to many (others); and we can consequently understand how it was that two sets of words, opposite in significance, were invented to mark the way in which the Carnival season was passed." There is no doubt considerable truth in this account, but it seems more likely that the words were adopted or adapted rather than expressly invented.

By the fifteenth and sixteenth centuries Carnival was celebrated throughout most of Europe, and the length of the festival tended always to increase. At first it was confined to Shrove Tuesday, then extended to three days, then a week, and so back and back till it immediately followed Christmas, which in some places lasted up to Candlemas, February 2, in others to January 6. And the Venetian Carnival, famous for its lavish splendour, began on what we would call Boxing Day, continuing undiminished all through January and February to the beginning of Lent.

"During this time of folly," an English traveller observed in 1756, "the better sort of company attend opera's, comedies and gaming houses . . . The common people divert themselves chiefly with rope-dancers, juglers, fortune-tellers, etc. . . .

There are also bull-baitings, goose-catchings, races of gondolas, fist-fightings, with several other diversions too tedious to enumerate . . . Married women under the protection of a mask enjoy all the diversions of the carnival, but are usually attended by the husband or his spies."

Moreover everyone was expected to appear in costume and the streets were full of

> . . . dresses splendid but fantastical,
> Masks of all times and nations, Turks and Jews,
> And harlequins and clowns, with feats gymnastical,
> Greeks, Romans, Yankee-doodles and Hindoos.

For, as our traveller goes on to remark, "the great diversion of the place is masquerading . . . The crowd of masqueraders is often so great in the piazza of S. Mark, that there is no passing; a man may take upon himself what character he pleases, so he be qualified to act the part he assumes." And as he wistfully adds, "these disguises give occasion to a vast number of adventures; there seems to be something more intriguing in the amours of Venice, than in those of other countries." Readers of *The Story of my Life* by Giacomo Casanova would not dispute this opinion.

Another writer to record what he witnessed at "Shrovetide, when all the world repaire to Venice to see the folly and madness of the Carnevall", was the diarist Evelyn. Though he feels he should disapprove his description is vivid and breathless, telling of "Women, Men & persons of all conditions disguising themselves in antique dresses, & extravagant Musique & a thousand gambols, & traversing the streets from house to house, all places being then accessible, & free to enter: There is abroad nothing but flinging of eggs fill'd with sweete Waters, & sometimes not over sweete: They also have a barbarous custome of hunting bulls about the Streetes & Piazzas, which is very dangerous, the passages being generally

so narrow in that Citty: Likewise do the youth of the several
Wards & Parrishes contend in other Masteries or pastimes,
so as 'tis altogether impossible to recount the universal madnesse of this place during this time of licence: Now are the
greate Banks set up for those who will play at Basset, the
Comedians have also liberty & the operas to exercise: Witty
Pasquils are likewise thrown about, & the Mountebanks have
their stages at every corner."

No wonder carnival, when it was used in England, came to
mean "any season or course of feasting, riotous revelry or
indulgence". In America, according to Webster, it can even
describe the kind of itinerant fair that moves from town to
town, "a travelling enterprise consisting of such amusements
as sideshows, games of chance, Ferris Wheels, merry-go-rounds
and shooting galleries." But these and our English carnivals,
often organised in summer by seaside resorts, with their fancy-
dresses, streamers, floats and Carnival Queens, are a very pale
reflection of what Carnival once was. Moreover their relation
to the season, their *raison d'être*, has entirely disappeared.

As for the famous *Hôtel Carnavalet* in Paris, where Madame
de Sevigné once lived and which is now a well-known museum,
its name, sad to say, has no connexion at all with *le carnaval*.
It is a French corruption of the title of a former owner,
Madame de Kernevenoy, who bought it in 1578, not long
after it was built.

In Venice some kind of "misguise" was imperative for the
Carnival, yet not everyone wanted to dress up. In this case
the accepted wear both for men and women was a long cloak
of black or grey (scarlet for the nobility), above it a close-
fitting short cape with a hood made of black silk reaching to
the waist, and a black velvet half-mask for the eyes. In later
times the cape or mantle grew longer and the cloak was dispensed with. So was born the famous costume known, for
what reason we cannot be sure, as the Venetian domino.

Both the word and the garment seem to have come from the Church. Cotgrave noted that in French *domino* meant "a kind of hood or habit for the head, worn by Cannons", that is, regular clergy who served a cathedral or a collegiate church. More specifically Littré tells us it was a robe which priests wore in winter over their surplices, having a piece of cloth to cover the head. The idea was clearly to give warmth in cold churches and monasteries; among the many apocryphal dying sayings attributed to the ex-friar, ex-monk François Rabelais is, "Put me on my domino, for I am cold; besides I would die in it." The point lies in the Latin text *beati mortui qui in Domino moriuntur*, blessed are the dead which die in the Lord.

Rather unhelpfully the *OED* says that domino in this sense is "derived in some way from the Latin *dominus*", a word which crops up in any number of disguises and always meaning master, ruler or lord; "the master of the *domus* or house is naturally the *dominus*". It was a title given to God himself, to his priests and to members of the ruling classes; it even descended to pedagogues, as in the Scots dominie and the English don. Thus Skeat's categoric statement that a domino was "originally a hood worn by a master" is of no help at all. Masters of Arts, it is true, wore distinguishing hoods and cloaks as part of their everyday costume, but all other writers associate the domino specifically with the Church.

A reasonable suggestion is that its name came from some Latin phrase or ecclesiastical formula, such as *Benedicamus Domino*, let us bless the Lord. It is tempting to imagine some old and rheumaticky canon kneeling in a stone-cold church and exclaiming "Blessed be God!" in gratitude for his nice warm woollen robe. And there is always the possibility that, as hoods and cloaks were generally worn when the Office was chanted in choir, the name came from its association with some such formula, daily and hourly repeated. According to Littré, however, this *vêtement de tête pour les prêtres* is related to *dominicale*, of the Lord, *dans le sens de coiffure qu'on mettait pour aller communier.* In other words it was worn expressly to partake of the body of the *Dominus*, the Lord.

In the seventeenth century a domino might be "a fashion of vaile used by some women that mourne", part of the widow's weeds. But it had also became firmly secularised as "a kind of loose cloak, apparently of Venetian origin, chiefly worn at masquerades, with a small mask covering the upper part of the face, by persons not personating a character." It is perhaps of interest that in 1730 Bailey defined *domino* as "the habit of a Venetian nobleman, very much in use at our modern masquerades". And Nugent, writing of the Carnival in Venice some years later, remarked that "those who only desire to be spectators take the habit of noblemen". There may be another connexion here with *dominus*, for noblemen and clerics in Italy, as in Spain, had the title Don, and *domino* was anciently used for lord or master both in Church and State.

That masquerades and the habit of attending them in long black Venetian robes were popular in eighteenth century England can be seen from *Tom Jones*, where the hero is sent by a fair unknown "a domino, a mask and a masquerade ticket" to equip him for an evening out. Here the word clearly describes the garment itself, which had by now most probably developed the long loose sleeves that made it more adaptable for dancing and other amusements. But once he put on his robe Tom Jones would think of himself as a domino and would so refer to anyone else he met in a similar costume. Moreover the small half-mask, here mentioned separately, was also known as a domino and so was a person wearing such a mask, as women of quality sometimes did when travelling.

Because of this it is not always easy to recognise what the word means in any given context. There is a story of Lady Mary Wortley Montague who in 1744 was invited to a great ball held at Nîmes during the Carnival in honour of the Duc de Richelieu. Because she was English and thus to them a Protestant, the persecuted Huguenots begged her to plead on their behalf with this minister of the King. Such a commission delighted her, and in her own words she decided she "would not therefore dress myselfe for the supper, but went in a Domine to the Ball, a Masque giving oppertunity (sic) of talking in a freer manner than I could have done without it." Though she seems to equate the domino with the mask, since she did not dress she must have meant the long loose costume; this is borne out by Horace Walpole's account of the same occasion: "A great masquerade being made . . . for Duc de Richelieu, (she) went to it in a dirty domino, talked to him for 3 hours . . . and returned without unmasking." One feels rather sorry for the Duke!

Dominoes of this kind lingered on in England till the early twentieth century. By then for most people the word meant something rather different—a simple, amusing game and the counters with which it was played. Why these dominoes were so called and whether they have any connexion with the Venetian domino remains a mystery. The whole of their story is almost as bedevilled with blanks as the dominoes themselves.

One thing at least seems certain, that the prototype of the domino was thought up by the Chinese. Our ordinary, excessively ancient six-sided cubic dice are said to have reached China from India thousands of years ago. In most games it is usual to throw not one but a pair of dice. On this idea the Chinese produced a refinement in the shape of little tablets of ivory, bone or wood, exquisitely carved and showing on their faces every possible combination of the numbers on two dice, for they had no blanks. With these bone tablets or *kwat p'ai* many complicated games could be played, among them *Ma-jong*, all the rage in England during the nineteen twenties and then suddenly dying overnight.

European dominoes, though differently designed, work on the

G

same principle as the Chinese *kwat p'ai*. And the European
game of dominoes seems to have been first played, as far as
we know, in Italy. Those who wish to preserve the continuity
of history maintain it was probably brought there "from China
by Marco Polo or some other traveller", or more vaguely that
it came "along the Venetian trade routes during the fifteenth
and sixteenth centuries".

Reasonable as these suggestions appear, they rest on no
solid foundations. They are simply attempts to provide a
direct link with Venice and her domino. And sad to say
Venetian trade with the East declined long before 1750, the
date lexicographers give for the word with its new meaning.
This does not, of course, imply that the game wasn't played
before then; merely that it hadn't attained definitive form
under any definite name.

A domino, then, is "one of a number of flat rectangular
pieces . . . having the underside black and the upper equally
divided by a cross line into two squares, each either blank
or marked with pips, so as to present all the possible combinations from double blank to double six", double blank
being the equivalent of the French *double blanc*—white. These
possible combinations number twenty-eight; some sets go up
to double nine, when there are fifty-two pieces, or double
twelve when there are eighty-five.

As most commonly enjoyed the game of dominoes begins by
each player being dealt or drawing a "hand". One piece is
placed face upward, the next man matches the number at
either end with a piece of his own, and so on round the table,
"placing corresponding ends in contact as long as this can
be done, the player who has the lowest number of pips remaining being the winner." But if a man was able to play out the
whole of his hand, he then cried "Domino!" to show he had
won the game.

If it has any rational meaning, does the name derive from

the cry or from the pieces? In more opulent times these were made with ivory faces and ebony backs, and it was said to be "the supposed resemblance of the black back of each of the pieces to the masquerade garment", acting perhaps as a sort of disguise for the numbers on the front, that gave them the name of dominoes. The Italian Battisti suggests it may perhaps come from the two colours white and black of the *maschera omonima*, the mask of the same name. Skeat says its origin is "the phrase *faire domino*, to complete (and win) the game", which tells us nothing at all. And Webster relates it back directly to "*dominus*, master, lord, exclamation of the winner".

All this is hearsay and not evidence. Hearsay too, but certainly worth repeating is the charming story Littré quotes of the origin of the game. It is found in the *Annuaire de l'Eure* and tells us the game of *domino* (singular in French and Italian) came about this way. Some monks belonging to the monastery of Monte Cassino, having been put in the penitential cell, beguiled their time by cutting out squares of wood, marking them with spots and playing a game with them. When they emerged from the cell they taught the game to the other monks; and every time one of the players succeeded in laying down all his squares he cried out, "*Benedicamus Domino!*", a customary formula with monks. So this domino often repeated became the name of the game.

This story has two points in its favour: it sets the scene in Italy and it accounts for the strange exclamation of the winner. But perhaps after all it is just a little too pat. The *Annuaire* rests its case upon "an old chronicle". Sceptically Littré asks which? No one seems to know.

Yet it is a matter of history that dominoes reached England in something the same kind of way. At the end of the eighteenth century our prisons were full of French soldiers captured during the long and tedious Napoleonic Wars. Like the monks they relieved their boredom by carving small models and toys which they sold to curious visitors, and probably these play-things included "squares of wood, marked with spots". Maybe they taught the game to their jailers, who took it home to their children. Certainly Strutt in 1801 thought of it as "a very childish sport, imported from France a few years back, and could have nothing but the novelty to recommend it to the notice of grown persons in this country." Though he doesn't specifically say so, he doubtless classed it among those "silly games, which are, I am told, frequently to be seen at low public houses, where many idle people resort and play at them for beer and trifling stakes of money."

In England it never became exactly fashionable and was for the most part "confined to the lower orders of Society". Disraeli in *The Young Duke* tells how "the menservants were initiated into the mystery of dominoes". Among the people, however, its popularity must have been wide, for the cry of "Domino!" passed almost at once into common speech, with the significance of a knock-out blow or a hopeless defeat. "I felt sure it was domino for me and my hopes," quotes Webster; that is, there was no hope for me, I was done for. And in the Army and the Navy in the days of Victoria completion of a punishment, the last lash of a flogging, was named the domino.

At one time too it could be heard in Cockney accents echoing through the London streets. "Probably," wrote a correspondent to *Notes and Queries* in 1882, "most Londoners have often heard 'bus conductors cry 'Domino' when an omnibus is 'full in and out'. Can explanation be given of this? Possibly it may be derived from the winner at the game of dominoes calling 'Domino', to signify that the game is won." Alas, none of the journal's erudite readers appears to have sent a reply; no doubt because his supposition was so evidently right.

9

WELCOME, MERRY SHROVETIDE

Coryat, visiting Italy about 1610, noted that "their Carnivall day . . . is observed amongst them in the same manner as our Shrove-Tuesday with us in England." Since Shrove-Tuesday now means little but pancakes his statement sounds wildly exaggerated. Yet it is recorded that at the Scottish court in 1480 "Fasteringis evin", an old name for the feast, "was celebrated . . . with tourneying, mumming and other festivities". According to Warton in the seventeenth century, "Shrove-Tide was formerly a season of extraordinary Sport and Feasting". And the *OED* has a verb, now obsolete, to shrove, meaning "to make merry", with a present participle shroving, "the keeping of Shrove-tide, the merrymaking characteristic of this season; festive rejoicing, carnival." So Coryat, it seems, was right.

Justice Silence was recalling youthful follies when, slightly in his cups, he sang:

'Tis merry in hall when beards wag all,
And welcome merry Shrovetide.

In England this season, unlike the Carnival, failed to prolong itself and was confined to three days, "the sondaye In Quinquagesime, with the tweyn dayes folowynge, that is clepyd Schroftide". And its strange and ancient name is peculiar to English.

Shrove Tuesday has had other names, marking it clearly as the beginning of Lent. In Gaelic it was called "Beginning Tuesday", *Di-Mairt Inid*, from Latin *initium*. In England it was commonly known as Fastens-eve or Fastens-een. Fasten, long obsolete, once meant "an act of fasting", and Fastens-een "the eve of or day before the fast (of Lent)". In Germany they call it *Fastnacht* or Fast Night, and the Munich Carnival, almost as riotous as once it was in Venice, is the *Fasching*. Here by tradition you are bound to spend all your money, then "go to the fountain on Ash Wednesday and wash out your empty purse". The local story is that *Fasching* derives not from fasting but from *fasen* or *faseln*, to talk nonsense, which at this time everybody does.

An even stranger version occurs in a Latin gloss of 1440, "Fast gonge or schroffetyde or gowtide, *carniprivium*". *Carniprivium* means the taking away of meat, and *gong* here is an old word for "an act of going", so presumably Fastgong or Fastingong signifies the approach of the Lenten fast. It crops up chiefly in East Anglia, so may have had a Danish origin. According to the civic records, in 1442 in Norwich a certain John Gladman "on Tuesday in the last ende of Christemesse, viz. Fastyngonge Tuesday, made a Disport with his Neyghbours, havyng his hors trappyd with tynne foile and other nyse disgisy things . . . and so rode in divers stretis of the cite with other people with him disguysed, makyng myrth, disportes and plays, coronned as Kyng of Crestemesse."

Such conduct was clearly not approved of. And this must have been one of the longest Christmasses on record. Easter that year fell on 1 April, and even Candlemas was over and gone by "Fastyngonge Tuesday". In 1674 "Fasguntide or Fastingtide" was still recorded as being the Norfolk name for "the time when the Fast of Lent begins", but by 1895 Walter Rye commented dryly, "The word, to do it justice, has something of a Saxon air, and may have been in use; indeed, may be so still, though inquiry has not detected it."

The northern and Scottish variation, Fastern's Een, survived much later. The date of this feast was calculated by an old rhyme:

> First comes Candlemas, then the new mune,
> The next Tuesday after is Fastern's E'en.

Sad to say this wasn't always in accord with the Church's method of fixing the date of Easter and working back from there, so the independent Scots often kept a Shrove-Tuesday of their own.

It is good Scots tradition that the man who "obtained (for them) from the Pope the knowledge that Shrove Tuesday was the first Tuesday of the first moon of Spring" was the thirteenth century scholar and wizard, Michael Scott. Dante put him among the "Diviners, Augurs and Sorcerers" in the Eighth Circle of Hell because "of a truth he knew the play of magic frauds",

> *Michele Scotto, che veramente*
> *Delle magiche frode seppe il gioco.*

Before this time the calculation of Easter was a closely guarded secret of the priests, and "a man left each country every year for Rome to ascertain the date of Shrove-tide". Michael Scott stopped all this by riding to Rome on the back of a devil and there making love to the Pope's daughter, in return for which questionable proceeding he "got the secret of the right date". No wonder Dante thought him the only Scot worthy of Hell!

Shrovetide, to return to the English name, is strange because of its unexpected spelling. It derives in some way from Old English *scrifan*, to shrive, a word now archaic if not obsolete, dying with the practice of confession. Shrove-tide, therefore, was the time for being shriven. The *OED* postulates a noun *scraf*, a shriving or confession, to account for shrove in Middle English, but such a word has never been found. Skeat and Partridge both think it is merely the past tense of the verb, which, being strong, gives shrive, shrove, as in drive, drove.

> Thanne Mede for here mysdedes to that man kneled,
> And shrove hire of hire shrewednesse,

wrote Langland. Since cattle are driven along a drove, it is possible that one who is shriven might go to shrove.

But the common word for confessing and receiving absolution was shrift, which still survives as a fossil in the phrase "short shrift". This once meant a brief respite, a breathing space, being literally applied to the "space of time allowed for a criminal to make his confession before execution". So when we give anyone short shrift we deal with them quickly, not allowing them much chance to put forward their side of the case.

That shrive should derive from *scrifan* is unexpected, for this is one of the great family descended from Latin *scribere*, which includes most European words for writers and writing and in English both scripture and scribe. With us, however, it had the primary sense of drawing up or writing down a law. Laws usually prescribe a penalty for those who break them, and from imposing a fine or suchlike punishment it was a short step to the imposition of a penance upon those who confessed their sins. When the priest dictated a penance he also gave absolution, so to shrive came to mean to absolve or to hear the confession of a penitent. Those, on the other hand, who made their confession and received absolution and penance took shrift, were shriven, or simply went to shrift: "Have you got leave to go to shrift today?" inquires the Nurse of Juliet, showing the word lived at least as long as the practice.

Good Catholics are still required to go to confession and

communion at least once a year, "at Easter or thereabouts". Why these islands should have adopted Shrovetide as expressly "the time for confessing and shriving" is not clear. But the serious nature of the obligation can be seen from Dunbar who in 1490 visualised defaulters as carried off to hell by Mahoun —that is Mohammed, here translated into a fiend:

> Me thocht, amangis the feyndis fell,
> Mahoun gart cry ane dance
> Off schrewis that wer nevir schrievin
> Aganiss the feist of Fasternis evin,
> To make their observance.

Once duty had been done, however, the rest of the day was free for "feasting and boisterous hilarity". For centuries, according to *British Calendar Customs*, Shrovetide was associated with "the making and eating of pancakes, door to door visits by children and others who sang to obtain Shrovetide gifts, football, games and sports," including cock-fighting and the even more barbarous pastime of throwing at a cock. As with the Carnival, the height of Shrovetide revelry came in the thirteenth, fourteenth and fifteenth centuries. Some of the traditional merry-making "survived the restraining efforts of the Reformers and the Puritans" and was "observed with enthusiasm" till the nineteenth. But by the twentieth "the making and eating of pancakes is one of the few customs left."

Thus Brand was not entirely correct when he said that "prior to the Reformation" Shrovetide was "a period of penitential observance . . . but at a later date was partly converted into a sort of holiday and carnival with the incidence of collops, pancakes, etc., and a variety of sports." What the Reformers did, as with so many of our feasts, was to destroy the religious content as idolatrous and popish. The festivities they suppressed but could not banish. In time these came back, now almost entirely divorced from the religion that once prompted them, only to be roundly condemned and denounced as pagan: "This furnyshing of our bellies with delicates, that we use on Fastingham Tuesday, what time some eate tyl they be forsed to forbeare all again, sprong of Bacchus Feastes, that were celebrated in Rome with great joy and deliciouse fare."

Some of the more exuberant descriptions of doings on Shrove Tuesday sound as if this might well be true. Perhaps the most eloquent comes from *Vox Graculi*, the Voice of the Jackdaw, published in the reign of James I: "Here must enter that wadling, stradling, bursten-gutted Carnifex of all Christendome, vulgarly enstiled Shrove Tuesday, but, more pertinently, sole Monarch of the Mouth, high Steward to the Stomach, chiefe Ganimede to the Guts, prime peere of the Pullets, first Favourite to the Frying pans, greatest Bashann to the Batterbowles, Protector of the Pancakes, first Founder of the Fritters, Baron of Bacon-flitch, Earle of Egge-baskets, etc. This corpulent commander of those chollericke things called cookes, will show himselfe to be but of ignoble education; for by his manners you may find him better fed than taught whenever he comes."

But there was more to Shrove Tuesday than eating and drinking. In London this was the time

> When mad brained Prentices, that no man feare,
>   O'erthrowe the dens of bawdie recreation.

There are many references in the seventeenth century to the so-called Shrove-prentices, who "take the lawe into their owne hands and do what they list", or as another writer calls them, "a nest of ruffianly fellows, who took upon them at Shrovetide the name of London Prentices, and in that character invaded houses of ill-fame."

Though they claimed to attack only brothels, no one was safe once they were out in the streets:

No matron olde nor sober man can freely by them come,
At home he must abide that will these wanton fellows shonne.

Rich as well as poor were afraid, and drove their carriages fast with "a hundred gingling bells" about their horses' necks and servants standing behind "well armed with whips". Even then they didn't escape the "ruffianly fellows", for

. . . sometimes legges or armes they breake, and horse and carte and all
They overthrow, with such a force they in their course do fall.
Much less they man nor child do spare, that meetes them in the way,
Nor they content themselves to use this madnesse all the daye
But even till midnight holde they on, their pastimes for to make,
Whereby they hinder men of sleepe and cause their heads to ake.

It has always been easy to find some excuse for rioting in the streets, but apart from the fun to be had bawdy houses sound a most unlikely target. The clue lies in Dekker's remark about taking "the lawe into their owne hands". According to Brand it was "formerly a custom for the peace-officers to make search after women of ill-fame on Shrove Tuesday and to confine them during the season of Lent," a somewhat drastic method of cleaning up the City for the period of penitence. The Shrovetide Prentices claimed to be trying to help them in the execution of their duty, though there seems little doubt which caused the more nuisance, the Prentices or the whores.

Yet even the victims of violence were less to be pitied than
the wretched Shrovetide Cocks, poor creatures "tied up and
pelted with sticks on Shrove Tuesday". Sir Roger L'Estrange
in 1692 denounced this "Cudgelling of Shroving-Cocks" as
"a Barbarous custom", yet nearly a century later Trusler could
write of "throwing at a cock, the universal Shrove-tide
amusement".

Basic procedure entailed tying a cord nine or ten yards long
to the leg of a cock. The cord was then fastened to a stake
or held by the owner, while sticks or cudgels were thrown at
the bird from a marked distance of about twenty-five paces.
For this a charge was made of "a halfpenny a shy", later
raised to "three shies or throws for twopence", and the player
"wins the cock if he can knock him down and run up and
catch him before the bird recovers his legs . . . Broomsticks
were generally used to shy with." Owners, who could do quite
well from nimble birds, would accustom them for weeks beforehand to avoiding sticks thrown at them and "the cock, if well
trained, eludes the blows for a long time".

Thus for our ancestors "a Shrovetide cock" was the equivalent of our "Aunt Sally", an idea or proposition put up
solely to be knocked down. "He does set up a Shrove-Tuesday
Cock, for everyone to throw at", wrote Pierce in 1697. Such
references continue well on into the eighteenth century and
so did the practice, surviving as late as 1860 in some country
districts in spite of being often "cried down" or expressly
forbidden by the town crier on his rounds. And others besides
the cock sometimes came to grief. In 1783 one of the broomsticks "pitched upon the head of . . . a youth about thirteen
years of age and killed him on the spot", whereon the pitcher
not surprisingly found himself pitched into prison to meditate
on his bad luck.

If this so-called sport had any more specific origin than
thoughtless cruelty all trace of it has long disappeared. Brand

quotes from a jest-book maintaining it had its rise "in an unlucky discovery of an adulterous amour by the crowing of a cock", but straightway dismisses the idea as "too ridiculous to merit a serious confrontation". Much the same could be said of various other suggestions. Sedley, for instance, in 1693 thought the cock was being "punish'd for Saint Peter's crime" of denying his Master, when "immediately, while he yet spake, the cock crew". Or again there is supposed to be some "allusion to the indignities offered by the Jews to the Saviour of the world before his crucifixion". Since "they spit in his face, and buffeted him; and others smote him with the palms of their hands", the connexion, to say the least, is a little far-fetched.

The unknown author of *Clemency to Brutes*, a pamphlet published in 1761 condemning cock-throwing as inhumane and "a shocking abuse of time", even more so as it was spent tormenting "the very creature which seems by nature intended for our remembrancer to improve it; the creature whose voice like a trumpet summoneth man forth to his labour in the morning, and admonisheth him of the flight of his most precious hours throughout the day"—surely a provocation in itself —is more historical. He believes the practice sprang from our endless wars with France, because "the cock has the misfortune to be called in Latin by the same word which signifies a French-man", that is, *gallus*. Hence, "our ingenious forefathers invented this emblematical way of expressing their derision of, and resentment towards that nation: and poor Monsieur at the stake was pelted by men and boys in a very rough and hostile manner." Sad to say, however, Frenchmen themselves had the same disgusting habit, which rather spoils his neat little pun.

The most generally accepted story is, as the same author tells us, "that the crowing of a cock prevented our Saxon ancestors from massacring their conquerors, another part of our ancestors, the Danes, on the morning of a Shrove Tuesday, while asleep in their beds." Nowadays, of course, we would like to forget we ever indulged in such very un-English behaviour. Especially as even outsiders protested at its barbarity, among them a "learned foreigner", possibly Erasmus, who sarcastically observed that "the English eat a certain cake on Shrove Tuesday, upon which they immediately run mad and kill their poor cocks."

These "certain cakes" were undoubtedly pancakes, made on Shrove Tuesday, it seems, from time immemorial. As described in *Pasquil's Palinodia*, published in 1634,

> It was the day whereon both rich and poore
> Are chiefly feasted with the self same dish,
> When every paunch, till it can hold no more,
> Is Fritter-fild, as well as heart can wish.
> It was the day when every kitchen reekes,
> And hungry bellies keepe a Iubile,
> When Flesh doth bid adue for divers weeks,
> And leaves old Ling to be his deputie.

About the word pancake, of course, there is nothing strange. It is simply "a thin flat cake, made of batter, fried in a pan", and is often, as the *OED* adds, "taken as a type of flatness". We have eaten pancakes at least since the fourteenth century, though sometimes under other names—"Pancake or fritter or flap-iacke" wrote John Taylor in 1634 and in 1641 Brome calls them "Flap-iackes and Pan-puddings".

Fritter is simply French *friture*, from Latin *frigere*, to fry— "a portion of batter . . . fried in oil, lard, etc." Pepys, who enjoyed his food, noted in 1664, "Home to dinner. It being Shrove Tuesday, had some very good fritters." At one time indeed he belonged to a singular institution known as the Shrove Tuesday Club, whose members met every year for a slap-up meal; in 1660 they had "a special good dinner, a leg of veal and bacon, two capons and sausages and fritters, and abundance of wine."

Flap-jacks were so called because it was the custom to "flap" them, or throw them up and catch them in the pan. Flap here means "to toss with a smart movement; to throw down suddenly," the sense being an echo of the sound. Halliwell records as a dialect phrase in 1847 "Flap a froize, to turn in the pan without touching it." This general flapping and tossing added much to the fun of the feast.

Yet though pancakes have been associated with Shrove Tuesday for centuries, the name Pancake Day is not recorded till 1825. And in Scotland they have their own traditions. There it is Brose Day or Bannock Day, the customary dishes being broth or brewis, "oatcake with boiling water or milk poured on it", and home made bread or scones, "usually un-leavened, flat and round or oval".

Brand notes, without explanation, that "pancakes or crum-cakes are said to have been eaten at Barking Nunnery before the Dissolution" on Shrove Tuesday, and this is odd, for crum-cakes sound more like bannocks than fritters. Possibly, however, they were a species of crumpet, "a soft cake made of flour, egg, milk, etc., baked on an iron plate". According to Brewer these were once known as crumple-ettes, "cakes with little crumples". But Onions connects the word with the "crompid cake" mentioned in Wyclif's Bible and called in the Authorised Version "a wafer of unleavened bread". Crompid here means "curled up, bent into a curve, as is usual with the cakes baked on a griddle or iron plate", and is related to an old Dutch *cromp*, crooked or bent.

Pancake eating too has many origins attributed to it. One of the most interesting, coming from Sherwood Forest, takes us back again to the time of the Danish invasions. When the Danes, it is said, reached the village of Linby in Nottingham-shire, the Saxon men "ran into the Forest, and the Danes took

H

the Saxon women to keep house for them: this happened just
before Lent, and the Saxon women, encouraged by their
fugitive lords, resolved to massacre the Danes on Ash Wednesday. Every woman who agreed to do this was to make pancakes
for dinner on Shrove Tuesday as a kind of pledge to fulfil her
vow. This was done, and the massacre took place the next day."
An unlikely story perhaps, yet recalling the tale of the cock
that crowed so untimely in a similar situation it seems possible
there may be in it some small grain of truth.

Selden, who sniffed out Romanism everywhere, was probably
more correct when he "saw in the practice a vestige of 'church
works' ". The ingenious Brewer maintains the pancakes were
"originally intended to be eaten after dinner to stay the
stomachs of those who went to be shriven," presuming apparently that there would be a queue and they would have a
long wait. But the explanation usually given is that the custom
arose "from the necessity in the past, when conditions of
fasting were more strict, of using up eggs and fat before the
beginning of Lent", since at one time *lacticinia* or dairy products were forbidden along with both meat and fish.

If this were so, however, pancake feasts would surely be
general throughout the Catholic Church, and they are not. It
was strangely the Eastern Churches who observed them or
something similar. "The Russes," noted Hakluyt, "begin their
Lent always eight weeks before Easter; the first week they
eat eggs, milk, cheese and butter, and make great cheer with
pancakes and such other things." In the Greek Orthodox
Church this is known as "the week of cheese fare", and Quin-
quagesima Sunday is "the Sunday of cheese fare", *e kyriake tes
tyrines.*

But only in England did they ring the Pancake Bell. This
"bell formerly rung on Shrove Tuesday at or about eleven in
the morning . . . is generally held to have been originally
the bell calling to confession." If so it was soon secularised to

become "the signal for the cessation of work and the beginning of the holiday". Young people swarmed into the streets, and pans, which had been at the ready, were put over the fire to heat, for the tongue of the great booming bell said plainly, "Pan on! Pan on!"

Indeed, according to Taylor, there were some who could not wait till eleven. His graphic description, written in 1620, of "Shrove Tuesday, at whose entrance in the morning all the whole kingdom is inquiet", confirms "the learned foreigner" who said the English used to "run mad". For as soon as "the clocke strikes eleven, which (by the help of a knavish sexton) is commonly before nine, then there is a bell rung cal'd the Pancake-bell, the sound whereof makes thousands of people distracted, and forgetful either of manners or humanity; then there is a thing called wheaten floure, which the cookes do mingle with water, egges, spice, and other tragicall, magicall inchantments, and then they put it little and little into a frying-pan of boiling suet, where it makes a confused dismal hissing . . . until at last, by the skill of the cooke, it is transformed into the form of a Flap-Jacke, cal'd a pancake, which ominous incantation the ignorant people doe devoure very greedily."

Nowadays, sad to say, we take life far more glumly. But there is one place at least where the Pancake Bell still rings, though its effects are rather different. A number of housewives wearing aprons and head-scarves and holding a pan in their hands run down the street from the market place of Olney to the village church, tossing their pancakes as they go, and the winner traditionally receives a kiss from the sexton, a prayer-book and a presentation frying-pan.

This is the local Pancake Race, said to date from 1445 and perhaps the last survivor of Shrove Tuesday's "extraordinary Sport" and "boisterous hilarity". No one knows how it started, but the popular legend is that an harassed housewife, all behind as usual, started to make her pancakes rather late that day. These pancakes, it is said, "would be eaten to sustain her, for she would have a long wait to be shriven". Alas, when the church bell rang they were not quite finished, "but she hurried off to her shriving, carrying her griddle and pancakes with her". As a story it does very well. One is only tempted to ask why, if she would have a long wait anyway, she needed to rush off!

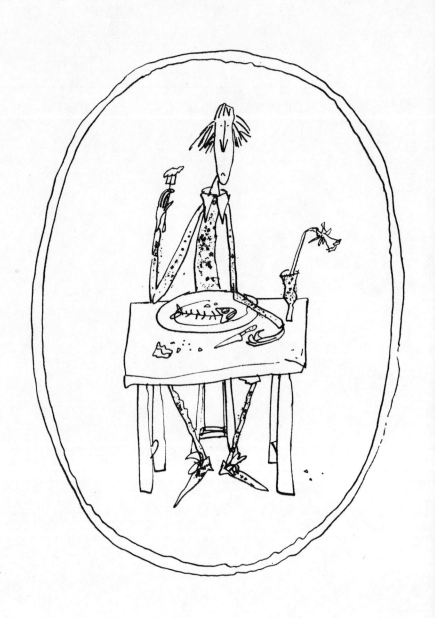

10

LENTEN YS COME

So begins an ancient anonymous English song, dated about
1300 and full of rejoicing:

> Lenten ys come with love to toune,
> With blosmen and with briddesroun,
>   That al blisse bryngeth;
> Dayes-eyes in this dales,
> Notes suete of nyhtegales,
>   Uch foul song singeth.

Surely this is not the mournful season of Lent, what Byron
described five centuries later as

> That penance which their holy rites prepare
> To shrive from man his weight of mortal sin,
> By daily abstinence and nightly prayer.

But the paradox is more apparent than real; the word has
simply changed its meaning. Lent, or more properly Lenten,
of which it is a shortening, was the old English name for
spring. "Sumer and lengten thu gescope hig", says the Anglo-
Saxon Bible; "thou hast made summer and spring." Lenten
was once *lencten*, related to an old High German *lengizen*,
and may have been derived from old Teutonic words such as
langi, long, and *tino*, a day. *Langitino* would thus refer "to
the lengthening of the days, as characterising the season of
spring". So Layamon in 1275 could say, "Thar after com
Leinten and dayes gonne longy."

John of Trevisa, writing of the equinoxes or the time when
day and night are equal (*equi*+*nox*=equal night) noted in 1387

that "the evenes of the day and of the nygt is ones in the
Lente, and efte in hervest." This is reminiscent of a Scottish
proverb, current until modern times:

> The Lenten even's lang and teuch,
> But the hairst even tummles owre the heuch.

Teuch is tedious, long drawn out; a *heuch* is a cliff. And the
gist of the saying is that "evenings in harvest are the same
length as in Lent, but seem to pass more quickly"—presumably
because of all the work there was to be done.

Trevisa's reference may be ambiguous, though he more
probably meant "the season of spring" than "the yeirlie
abstinence of fourty dayis afore Pasche, callit Lentren". This
time of penance became known as the *lencten-faesten*, later
shortened to Lent, simply because it occurred in the spring
when the days "gonne longy", and the use is peculiar to
English. Though Dutch *lente* can still mean the spring, Lent
is *Vastentijd*, fasting-time, as in the German *Fastenzeit*.

From the history of Lent, which is long and complicated, it
seems that at first it had no special name, being simply a
period of preparation "for the passion, death and resurrection
of Christ and a time of penitence, prayer and fasting, spiritual
and physical." In 195 Irenaeus speaks of some fasting for one
day, others for two, and still others for "forty hours of night
and day". Forty has always been a number of deep mystical
significance, and these forty hours were supposed to correspond
to the time when Christ lay in the tomb, the days "when the
bride-groom is taken away". In this case the fast was absolute.
About a century later, when it was extended to cover the whole
of Holy Week, Hippolytus recommended eating nothing but
"bread, salt and water". And already there is mention of a
forty-day fast on the grounds that "Our Lord and Moses and
Elijah fasted for that period".

Eventually the forty days, called in Greek *Tessarakoste* and in Latin *Quadragesima*, were adopted by the Council of Nicea in 325. Fasting began on the fortieth day (*quadragesima dies*) before Easter, still liturgically known as Quadragesima Sunday, and continued till Easter Eve. As all Sundays are feast days, however, *ipso facto* they cannot be fasts, which made the time of fasting thirty-six days only. For this reason in the seventh century four extra days were added, pushing back the start of the fast to the previous Wednesday. Since then what the OED describes as "the period including forty week-days extending from Ash Wednesday to Easter-Eve, observed as a time of fasting and penitence, in commemoration of our Lord's fasting in the wilderness", has remained unchanged.

Quadragesima or Quadragesime, which means merely "forti-eth", the ancient name for this time of penance, is echoed in most of the modern Romance languages—Italian *quaresima*, Spanish *cuaresma*, Old French *quaresme*, developing into *carême*, even Irish *corghas*, Scots Gaelic *carghus* and Welsh *garawys*. But our only use of it seems to have been for the Quadragesimalia or Lent offerings—"Quadragesimils," Bailey explains in 1721, are "Mid-Lent contributions, offerings made by the People to their Mother Church on Mid-Lent Sunday." What we English would have made of it if we had naturalised it we shall never know. Perhaps something like the obsolete *carene*, which did in fact mean "a forty days fast", or the longer *carentane* or quarantine, both signifying a period of forty days. But these have a slightly different derivation, and anyway we decided to be lazy and opt for Lent.

Rules of fasting for these forty days were at first extremely strict. Only one meal a day was allowed, originally not before three in the afternoon but gradually put forward to twelve. Flesh-meat and fish were absolutely forbidden, so were eggs and milk, butter and cheese. Not much remains except bread, fruit and vegetables and these, in England at least, were at their most scarce in Lent.

Everyone, unless dispensed or excused on the grounds of sickness or age, was expected to keep the fast. As time went on, however, more and more relaxations were made. By the Middle Ages fish was allowed almost everywhere, and during the fifteenth century milk and milk products were also generally permitted, so that abstinence in fact came to mean not eating meat.

What was known as lenten-stuff, or "provisions suitable for Lent", therefore, varied very much. According to Littré these *provisions de carême* included butter, oil, vegetables, dried fruits, salted fish, and other similar foods. Among the English, according to *British Calendar Customs*, "abstention from butcher's meat" resulted in what sounds like a feast of somewhat oddly chosen ingredients—"fish of many kinds, fritters, frumenty, figs, simnel and other cakes, cheese and cheese cakes, eggs, peas and radishes."

Fish, in the days before rapid transport and refrigeration, had to be usually salted, cured or dried—herrings, "old ling" and stock fish, "cod split and dried in the sun without salt", were almost synonymous with Lent. When John Gladman rode through Norwich on that famous "Fastyngonge Tuesday" some of the neighbours who accompanied him "makying myrth, disportes and plays" were dressed to represent the times and seasons. Among these came "Lenton clad in whyte and red heryng skinns, and his hors trappyd with oyster shells".

Indeed the onset of Lent was heralded, as Neogeorgus tells us, by the appearance in the streets of men who

> . . . beare about a herring on a staffe, and loude doe roare,
> Herrings, herrings, stincking herrings, puddings now no
> more.

Puddings were, of course, made of meat and therefore forbidden. And even dried fish wasn't very cheap, so only those fairly well off could indulge in it:

Both ling and saltfish they devoure, and fishe of every sorte,
Whose purse is full, and such as live in great and wealthy
    porte;
But onyans, browne bread, leekes and salt must poore men
    daily gnaw,
And fry their oten cakes in oyle,

since neither butter nor dripping was permitted.

After the Reformation Lent remained a part of the Church's year, though the earlier strict rules were relaxed and it was thought of more as a time of spiritual penance than of material fasting. With an eye to the national economy, however, both Elizabeth and James I issued proclamations, said to have been "vigorously enforced", which "ordered abstinence from flesh-meat on fast days" in order that "the fish and shipping trades might be benefited". Perhaps it is because of this that "fish on Friday" has been something of an English institution long after the Anglican Church allowed the eating of meat. There is indeed a sad heart-cry from Pepys on 10 March 1661— "Dined at home on a poor Lenten dinner of coleworts and bacon." But in spite of the cabbage he hadn't much ground for complaint; a few centuries earlier he might have done much worse.

As to the fish-trade, Cornishmen once raised their glasses with a toast during Lent of "Long life to the Pope and death to thousands". The thousands were pilchards, of which there was a "a large exportation . . . (at) this season, to Spain, Italy and other Catholic countries". Recent Popes have been less popular with fishermen since they have abolished all compulsory fasting and abstinence except on two days in the year.

In Lent people were expected to be sober and serious and not to enjoy themselves. From the first "entertainments, horse-racing and similar shows" were forbidden, so was dancing and cheerful conversation—"there should be no jesting on a fast day", so the rule ran. Some even adopted curious outward signs of mourning; it was noted in England as late as 1816 that "it is still the custom with some old people to wear black during Lent, and the clergy of the Established Church usually go without powder at this season"—powder, of course, on the hair, not on the face.

Weddings too were frowned on and Nuptial Masses not permitted for those that actually took place. The old proverb lingered long—"Marry in Lent and you'll live to repent." This was accounted for in 1876 by "the double fees and the ill-luck supposed to follow a couple united during the penitential forty days". But there are simpler reasons. A Lenten marriage was almost certain to be hasty, either against parental opposition or because a child was on the way and the couple could not wait. It has in fact the same force as the commoner saying, "Marry in haste, at leisure repent", still sometimes heard quoted today.

Lenten, before it was shortened to Lent, could be both a noun and an adjective and soon, because of its form, lost its nominal use completely. Narrowly it had the meaning "such as is appropriate to Lent, hence of provisions, diet, etc. . . . meagre." So Rosencranz tells Hamlet that the players will receive from him "Lenten entertainment", since "you delight not in Man". Later it was extended to describe "clothing, expression of countenance, etc., mournful-looking, dismal".

Thus a lenten-faced man was one "lean and dismal of countenance", liable to be addressed as "lenten-chaps, contemptuously applied to a person with a lean visage". But though the northern form of lenten was lentren or lenterne, there is no evidence that lantern-jawed means anything more than what it says—"thin-visaged, from their cheeks being almost transparent", as if a light would show through. None the less Grose in the eighteenth century rather pleasingly thought there might be some confusion with "lenten jawed; i.e., having the jaws of one emaciated by a too rigid observance of Lent."

There are other words where the association seems to be with the spring rather than with Lent. Such, for instance, is lenten-corn, what we would call spring corn, grain sown in the spring; this usage is recorded in *The Times* as late as 1901. Then the daffodil, which was once affodil or asphodel, has had for centuries the by-name of lent or lenten lily. Tennyson uses it, and Housman:

> And there's the Lenten lily
> That has not long to stay
> And dies on Easter day.

Some words, still older, have vanished with what they described. In the north, where lambing was late and often hard, lambs that "died soon after being dropped" were called lentrins and their skins known as lentrinware or lentenware. Falconers too would speak of lentners or lentiners, "the which," as Turbye explained in 1575, "are called with us March Hawkes or Lentiners, by cause they are taken in Lent with lime or such like means." Young birds for training were usually removed from the nest, but the popular peregrine falcons built on such steep and inaccessible crags that fledglings had to be caught on the wing "by nets, snares or other traps", as they flew away from the breeding-grounds. Hence their name of passage-hawks, peregrines—those who wander—or lentners, from the time when they were trapped.

Various other combinations apply more directly to the season. Lenten-fig, for instance, described by Cotgrave as "*Figue de Caresme*, a drie fig", or even a raisin; lenten-kail, which is "broth made without meat"; and the famous lenten-pie with which Mercutio teases the Nurse. "So ho!" he cries, like a huntsman coursing a hare, then announces he has found "no hare, sir; unless a hare, sir, in a lenten pie, that is something stale and hoar ere it be spent."

This is not the place to consider what Partridge calls "Shakespeare's bawdy"; sufficient to say that a hare has no business in a lenten-pie, which should contain no meat. Dover Wilson suggests its meaning here is "perhaps meat-pie consumed bit by bit surreptitiously in Lent and therefore mouldy (hoar) before it is all eaten." Indeed it could have been eaten openly on Sundays, but this, I feel, was scarcely Shakespeare's point.

One strange and unexplained allusion is to the lenten-top or "whirligigge" as John Taylor calls it. Even the omniscient *OED* can only suppose it was "some kind of toy used at Shrovetide." If so the tradition has persisted, for the Opies have noted how even in the present century on Shrove Tuesday schoolgirls brought out their skipping ropes and schoolboys their tops.

In a different category is the lenten-veil or lenten-cloth, "a curtain hung between the people and the altar during Lent in the Middle Ages, symbolising the expulsion of sinners and penitents from the Church according to ancient discipline." This was first white, then purple, the penitential colour, and sometimes, it seems, depicted what sounds like a last Judgement or a Doom:

> The images and pictures now are coverede secretlie
> In every Church, and from the beams, the roof and rafters hie,
> Hanges painted linen clothes that to the people doth declare
> The wrathe and furie great of God, and times that fasted are.

In Catholic churches statues, pictures and crucifixes are still hidden during Passion Week by purple veils, removed with great rejoicing at the first Mass of Easter. In the Sarum Accounts of 1546 one item reads, "vij yardes of Oscon brigges (a kind of satin) for to make seynt Thomas a lenton clothe at iiij d the yarde." The statue must have been of quite considerable size;

seven yards would make a bedspread and all for two and fourpence.

But there was amusement to be had even at the beginning of Lent, when at one time on Ash Wednesday

> Jake à Lent comes justlynge in,
> With the hedpeece of a herynge,
> And saythe, repent yowe of yower syn,
> For shame, syrs, leve yower swerynge:
> And to Palm Sunday doethe he ryde,
> With sprots and herryngs by hys syde,
> And makes an end of Lenton tyde.

This Jack o' Lent, "a ridiculous figure of a man made of straw and old clothes", rather like the more modern Guy, was carried through the streets with great hilarity and "thrown at, kicked, burnt and subjected to all kinds of rough treatment". The image was frequently said to represent Judas, and though the whole procedure more probably derives from spring festivals far more ancient than Iscariot the name and the connexion were widespread and very persistent.

As late as 1950 the Opies recorded the burning of Judas in parts of Liverpool, a city with a high Catholic population, though the date was changed to Good Friday. Children rose early and carried about a figure "with a comic mask for a face and dressed in an old suit of clothes". This was hoisted on a pole at first light and banged against bedroom windows with the cry, "Judas is a penny short of his breakfast," which penny each householder was expected to provide. When no more money seemed forthcoming the poor stuffed man was burnt. Tradition in Liverpool says this custom derived from "the effigies seen during Holy Week on board the old Spanish ships which docked and discharged their cargoes of wine and citrus fruits in the South End Docks." All the same it sounds very like a survival of the old Jack o' Lent.

A more probable explanation of his appearance comes from Germany, where "a ragged scarecrow used to personify Lent" was carried round the streets, or from Spain and Italy, where "a personification of the Carnival was sentenced to death and stoned, burned or drowned on Ash Wednesday." In France too, Carnival was solemnly interred "as a symbol of the burial of good living during Lent", an image representing good cheer being "carried around and money collected for its funeral". As Wright remarks, "whatever the origin of the Jack o' Lent custom, one of its objects was to show regret and annoyance at the advent of a period of abstinence and restraint after a season of feasting and amusement."

Unlike his Continental cousins, the English Jack o' Lent instead of being shot, burned, drowned or buried at once, remained on show until Easter, during which time he was pelted with sticks and stones; indeed the *OED* calls it "an ancient form of Aunt Sally, practised in Lent". If we are to believe Ben Jonson a man could even make money by taking on the job himself:

> Thou, that when last thou wert put out of service,
> Travell'dst to Hampstead Heath on an Ash Wednesday
> Where thou didst stand six weeks the Jack of Lent,
> For boys to hurl, three throws a penny at thee,
> To make thee a purse.

Quite naturally, therefore, the phrase came to mean both literally and metaphorically "a butt for everyone to throw at". It could also describe, before it died out of use, "an insignificant or contemptible person" and even "a scarecrow of old clothes, sometimes stuffed":

> How like a Jack a Lent
> He stands, for boys to spend their Shrovetide throes,
> Or like a puppet made to frighten crows.

Lent, it seems, was a time to be forgotten, not remembered; it has given us no personal names or none that I can trace, except for the surname Lentner. France, however, produced the redoubtable Marie-Antoine Carême, the great nineteenth century chef who served first Talleyrand, then the Tsar of Russia, then our own Prince Regent and finally James de Rothschild. Surely no cook could have a less appropriate name than "Mister Lent"!

THE DEATH DAY OF THE EGGS

Though Easter, the oldest Christian observance, "the feast of feasts and most solemn of all solemnities", commemorates yearly the resurrection of Christ, there is nothing about its name to show this except in the liturgical calendar where it is known as *Dominica Resurrectionis*, Resurrection Sunday. Even here the following days are described as "of the Pasch", the next Sunday being *Octava Paschae*, the octave of the Pasch.

Now this Pasch, "a name formerly in fairly wide currency in English both for the Jewish Passover and the Christian festival of Easter", represents Old French *pasche*, from Latin *pascha*, a transliteration of Greek *pascha*, which is again a transliteration of Hebrew *pesach* or *pesakh*. This word, meaning a passage or a passing over, denoted a Jewish festival celebrated every spring on the fourteenth day of the month Nisan, in commemoration "of the passing over of the houses of the Israelites, whose doorposts were marked with the blood of a lamb, when the Egyptians were smitten with the death of their firstborn." Immediately afterwards Moses led his people "out of the land of Egypt, out of the house of bondage", and Pesach was an occasion for rejoicing at this deliverance from captivity.

Essentially the feast involved the sacrifice of a lamb and a communal or family meal. There are some who say this offering of a lamb was merely a fertility rite, first practised at the time when the Israelites were a wandering pastoral people. Sacrifice was made of the first lamb of the season, its flesh "eaten as an act of communion with the god, and blood smeared to protect houses and flocks from evil". It has indeed been categorically said that "pasch means jump and probably referred to the tribal dance accompanying the sacrifice."

If this is so, the festival acquired a new meaning from being celebrated at the time of the Exodus. Instructions were given to Moses that each family should roast a lamb and eat it with unleavened bread and bitter herbs or, as the Douai says, wild lettuce. This meal was to be eaten in haste, "with your loins girded, your shoes on your feet, and your staff in your hand." But first the lintel of each door must be marked with blood, "for I will pass through the land of Egypt this night, and will smite all the firstborn in the land . . . and when I see the blood I will pass over you, and the plague shall not be upon you." In this way "the destruction of the Egyptians 'jumped' or passed over the Hebrew houses marked with blood", hence the name Pesach.

The meaning of this word, it seems, also includes the idea of sparing and protecting. And the Israelites, when asked by their children in after years why a lamb was still sacrificed yearly, were instructed to reply, in the Douai version, "It is the victim of the passage of the Lord, when he passed over the houses of the children of Israel in Egypt, striking the Egyptians and saving our houses."

In New Testament times the feast of Pesach remained the most important of the year. It was celebrated by whole families or by groups of from ten to twenty people. On the 14th day of Nisan lambs were ceremonially killed in the Temple, then taken home and roasted. Each of the guests brought four cups of red wine and the lamb was eaten with bitter herbs and unleavened bread or "passover cakes". One concession had been made, however; the meal was no longer taken standing but "recumbent, as a token, according to the Pharisees, of the rest which God hath given his people". More probably they were simply following the common Roman custom of reclining at banquets; this does at least make the idea of John "leaning on Jesus' bosom" sound a little less as if he were drunk.

For it was Pesach that Christ and his disciples were keeping at the Last Supper. And because the crucifixion, death and resurrection of Christ took place, by historical accident or deep religious fitness, at this time, the feast was once again transformed. Though John the Baptist first called Christ *Agnus Dei*, Lamb of God, it was Saint Paul who gave most Christians their word for Easter when he told the Corinthians to celebrate the feast not "with the leaven of malice and wickedness, but with the unleavened bread of sincerity and truth . . . for Christ our passover is sacrificed for us"—*etenim pascha nostrum immolatus est Christus*. Here *pascha* means not the feast but the sacrificial lamb—"Christ is the true lamb . . . who by dying has overcome our death and by rising again has restored our life." *Pesach* in Aramaic was *paskha*, becoming in Saint Paul's Greek *pascha*; for him Passover and Easter shared a name. So they do in French *pasche*, later *Pâques*, in Italian *Pasqua*, in Spanish *Pascua*, in Dutch *Pask*. But not in English, or not at least in common speech; we have our own words for both.

Passover, peculiarly English, owes its origin to the translators of the Bible and its popular currency to the Reformation. In England, as in other countries, Latin *pascha* was at first generally used, written pasche, pask or even phask. Thus Ormin, a thirteenth century exponent of reformed spelling, explained:

> Forr Passke—yiff thu turnenn willt
> That word till Ennglissh spaeche,
> Tha taccneth itt tatt uss birrth ayy
> Uss flittenn toward Christe,

meaning briefly if you turn Pask into English speech you show what carries us struggling towards Christ. Or, as a later writer more explicitly states, "That nigt sal ben fest pasche, forth-for, on Engle tunge it be." Forth-for, to interpret his interpretation, is "a going forth, departure, death".

The emphasis here is much more on the idea of a journey than of sparing or passing over. Wyclif in 1382 is non-committal; he uses in one place the odd spelling phask, which seems to have come from an error in the Latin of the Vulgate, but in Mark 14 the disciples preparing the feast are instructed to ask, "Wher is my fulfilling (or etyng place) where I schal ete pask?" It seems to have been Tindale in 1530 who first spoke of "the Lordes passeover" and in this he was followed by Coverdale. The Douai translation of 1582 reverted to pasch, or in Exodus "the Phase (that is the Passage) of the Lord". This too is part of an old tradition, for Trevisa in 1398 wrote that "Ester is callyd in Ebrew Phase, that is passynge other passage". The Authorised Version, however, opted firmly for Passover and the earlier variants thereupon disappeared.

Wyclif, rather strangely, changed his mind in later editions and substituted Easter for pask, on the ground that the latter would not be "understanded of the people". And in one place at least the confusion still remains. For we read in Acts of the 1611 Bible that Herod apprehended Peter and left him in prison during "the days of unleavened bread . . . intending after Easter to bring him forth to the people."

Yet Easter, though in name entirely pagan, now describes only the Christian feast of the Resurrection. Many explanations of the origin of this word have been put forward; that generally accepted is the earliest, given by Bede a thousand years ago. Writing of April he says it was called "Eosturmonath, which is now rendered the Paschal month, and formerly received its name from a goddess (worshipped by the Saxons and other ancient nations of the north) called Eostre, in whose honour they observed a festival in this month. From the name of this goddess they now design the Paschal season, giving a name to the joys of a new solemnity from a term familiarized by the use of former ages." When he came to England Saint Augustine is said to have been advised by Pope Gregory to "accommodate the ceremonies of the Christian worship as much as possible to those of the heathen, that the people might not be too much startled by the change," and he seems to have followed his instructions to the letter.

The Germans have a similar name for this season—*Ostern* or *Osterfest*, deriving apparently from Ostara, another version of Eostre. According to Brand, however, the feast was "so called from the Saxon *oster*, to rise", which would be beautifully simple if only someone had proved that *oster* with this meaning existed. A certain Herr Wachter, indeed, whose national pride, says Jamieson, was "hurt at the idea of the Germans, after they had embraced Christianity, retaining the name of a heathen deity for . . . one of their principal feasts," tried to connect it with *urstend* or *urständ*, resurrection. Though words are subject to many strange transformations, this one seems unlikely; especially as the Anglo-Saxon equivalent verb was *astanden*, as remote from Easter as *urständ* from *Ostern*.

Other students of language have made even wilder suggestions; that Easter comes from *styrian*, to put in motion, or from the Anglo-Saxon *yst*, a storm, "the time of Easter", explains Brand, "being subject to the continual recurrence of tempestuous weather". But an unnamed priest whose *Sermo Brevis* was recorded in the reign of Henry VI had no doubt at all upon the subject: "Gode men and wommen, as ye knowe alle welle, this day is called in some place Astur Day, and in some place Pasch Day, and in some place Goddus Sunday. Hit is callde Asturday . . . for wolnoy in uche place hit is the maner this day for to done fyre oute of the houce at the Astur that hath bene all the wynter brente wyt fyre and blakud with smoke, hit schal this day bene arayed with grene rusches and swete floures strowde alle aboute . . . rygte so ye scholde clanson the houce of youre sowle." The *astur* is the hearth, and Easter here is interpreted as Hearth Day, the day for clearing out all the accumulated soot of the winter and strewing fresh rushes on the floor—spring-cleaning, in fact. The moral transference is obvious.

However we still return to Bede and the "very early Teutonic goddess of spring" called Eostre, "whose festival was celebrated at the vernal equinox", and who was herself connected with ideas of rising and new life. For though little is known about her cult it seems likely she was once a dawn goddess, related to the Latin Aurora and to what C. M. Yonge calls "Greek Hos, the goddess who unbarred the gate of the day". In ancient Sanskrit the word for dawn was *usra* and from it almost certainly come both Easter and east, the direction where the sun is known to rise. Since spring, with its increasing light and warmth, is "the dawn of the living year", it was natural a dawn goddess should be worshipped at this season. According to Partridge, however, the basic idea behind *usra* is "it dawns, it shines". Eostre therefore emerges as the goddess of spring because "after dull winter (it) comes as 'the shining season' ".

Easter, then, established itself very early as the popular title of *Dominica Resurrectionis* or God's Sunday, since even to Bede its pagan associations are merely historical. Yet rather surprisingly it never gained any general acceptance as a personal name. In France Easter children were baptized Pasquin, Pasquier or Pascal, in Italy Pasquale or Paschino, in Spain Pascual. Here Easter does occur, but only rarely, either as a surname or given name. C. M. Yonge records an instance in Ripon Cathedral in 1813, and also notes that she saw it written in a prayerbook, but adds in both cases it may be "a mistake for Esther", which represents Hebrew *Hadassah*, a myrtle, and is no relation. Certainly where it is found, together with the pet name Eacy, it is always feminine; at least to this extent the goddess held her own. Indeed she still does, for only recently I heard of an Easter daughter being christened Eostre.

In place-names, however, Easter seldom means what it says. Usually it represents either Anglo-Saxon *eastor*, eastern, or *easterra*, more eastern, as in Easterford (eastern ford), Eastergate (eastern gate), Asterley (eastern or more eastern field). And Osterley is said to derive from quite a different word *eowestre*, a sheep-fold. This occurs again in the romantically named High Easter and Good Easter, which mean no more than the high sheepfold and the sheepfold belonging, so local records say, to the lady Godgiefu or Godiva.

For centuries side by side with Easter the Latin *pascha*, spelt usually pasch or paske, was also current in English. The Anglo-Saxon Chronicle records that in 1131 "king Heanri on this yeare waes on Pasche on Norhthamtune", and a Catechism of 1357 lays down the rule that Christians should communicate at least "anes in the yhere, that is to say, at paskes". Caxton in 1481 writes of "the feste of ester or pasque", and this usage survived at least until the seventeenth century. In his *Scottish Dictionary* Jamieson calls Easter "a foreign word" and states that it did not appear in Scots until the union of the Crowns in the reign of James the First and Sixth. Before then the feast was called Pasch, Paiss, Pays, Pace or even Peace Sunday, though in Gaelic it sometimes had locally the rather charming title of *Bas nan Uibhean*, the death day of the eggs.

Thus a boy born at Easter might be called Pask or Pascal (pertaining to Easter), or if he lived in Cornwall, Pascoe. Though these names in later times were rare they must once have had wide currency because of the number of surnames associated or probably associated with them. Pascall, Paskell and Pasquill are obvious Easter names; so are Pask and Paish, and possibly Patchett and Patch. Pace and even Peace may have the same derivation, or they may come from Latin *pax*, peace, via an earlier pais. Pacey may belong to this family or it may not. For there seems to have been a Saxon tribe called the Paecci or people of Pacca who left their mark on many places names such as Pakefield and even Pachesham which look as if they ought to belong to Easter. It is all, to put it mildly, a little confused.

There is in modern English, however, one definite use remaining of the old title of Easter—the name of the Pasque or pasch-flower, a kind of anemone. It was so called by John Gerarde who described it in his *Herball or generall Historie of Plantes*, published in 1597. "It hath," he says, "many small leaves finely cut or jagged, like those of Carrots; among which rise up naked stalkes, rough and hairie; whereupon doe grow beautiful floures bell fashion, of a bright delaied[1] purple colour", commonly known "after the Latine name *Pulsatilla* or Flaw floure", both of which indicate its habit of nodding in the breeze. *Pulsatilla* comes from *pulsare*, to strike or beat; a flaw is "a sudden burst or squall of winde" so flaw-flower is the same as wind-flower, the usual name of the wild anemone.

This plant, explains Gerarde, has no specific medical uses; "there is nothing extant in writing among Authors of peculiar vertue, but they serve only for the adorning of gardens and garlands, being floures of great beautie." Perhaps for this reason it was called in French *passe-fleur, ainsi dit*, says Littré, *parce-qu'il passe les autres fleurs*. Gerarde records this name and in a moment of inspiration decides to alter it, since "they floure for the most part about Easter, which has mooved mee to name it Pasque Floure or Easter floure". And so it has been called ever since.

The old herbalist clearly loved the flowers in spite of their lack of "vertue", relating how they "do grow very plentifully in the pasture or close belonging to the parsonage house of a small village six miles from Cambridge, called Hildersham. The Parson's name . . . was Mr. Fuller, a very kind and loving man, and willing to show unto any man the said close, who desired the same." Here in Hildersham, it seems, they had

[1] pale or diluted.

another name, "Couentrie bels", but the reason for this is obscure. In Cambridgeshire, after three centuries, they still grow wild, but no one, so far as I know, calls them Coventry bells.

The word Easter can of course be used to describe Easter eggs or Easter bonnets; in more learned contexts we have a parallel adjective paschal, from Latin *paschalis*. Paschal time extends after Easter for fifty-six days until the Saturday after Whitsun. During these weeks in Catholic churches the Paschal candle burns, "a large candle blessed and lighted in the service of Holy Saturday and placed on the Gospel side of the altar, there to remain till Ascension Day." Commonly referred to as the Paschal, it represents the *Lumen Cristi gloriose resurgentis*, the light of Christ risen in glory:

> A taper great, the Paschall namde, with music then they bless,
> And frankincence herein they pricke, for greater holynesse,
> This burneth night and day as signe of Christ that conquered hell.

Some indeed took this literally; according to Jeremy Taylor, "they then thought that when the Paschall taper burn'd, the flames of hell could not burn, till the holy wax was spent."

These candles, made of "the wax of bees" which has "always been regarded as a type of the pure flesh of Jesus", at one time were vast and impressive. The great Easter taper at Westminster is said to have been of "three hundred pounds weight", and at Durham it was "square wax, and reached to within a man's length of the roof". But not all this was candle; there was also a "canstick", equally known as a paschal. Thus the Durham Ritual of 1593 records that "on the height of the candlestick or pascall of lattine (a yellow alloy similar to brass) was a faire large flower . . . wherein did stand a long peece of wood . . . whereon stood a great long square taper of wax called the paschall."

Often this candlestick had seven branches, the middle one, the "long peece of wood" on which the candle was actually placed, being known as the Judas or Judas of the Paschal. In 1453 the Coventry Accounts record provision of "iiij newe torches & iiij judasses", and at Reading in 1520, "For makyng a Judas for the Pascale 1d." But what its association with Iscariot and how it got this name I do not know.

Unlike most other feasts, Easter appears to have no set traditional meal, unless it be roast lamb and tansy pudding. Aubrey, it is true, records that in the seventeenth century there was always placed on the table "a red herring riding away on horseback, i.e. arranged to look something like a man on horseback and set in a corn salad." But this was merely a symbolic farewell to Lent and the fish-eating season. No one, I am sure, ate the herring; no one wanted even to think about fish for weeks to come. The French indeed have a saying that a man who undertakes an enterprise when there is little call for the services he offers *se fait poissonnier la vieille de Pâques*, sets up as a fishmonger on the eve of Easter.

What everybody eats at Easter is, of course, eggs. And our Easter eggs, though efforts have been made to baptise them, are pagan symbols of great antiquity. Thousands of years ago, it is said, the Greeks and Romans, the Persians and the Chinese exchanged coloured eggs at the Spring Festival. They typify rebirth, fertility, continuing life, the flowering of spring out of winter. Some writers identify Eostre with Ishtar, the Babylonian goddess of fertility; in this they are firmly, though perhaps unwittingly, supported by the charming bunnies that still appear on our Easter cards, the Easter rabbits and the Easter hares.

Jokes about the breeding propensities of rabbits are immemorial; for centuries they have been regarded as a symbol of fertility and increase. Hares, and maybe rabbits as well, were sacred to Eostre in her capacity of goddess of the spring.

This may account for the strange tradition, dying very hard, that Easter eggs were laid or brought not by hens but by hares. For this reason too in paintings of Venus there are often rabbits at play on the flower-strewn grass about her feet.

A later and more sentimental story associates these eggs with the Easter bells. The last three days before Easter were at one time known as the Swidages or silent days, just as Good Friday in German is *der stille Freitag*. During this holy time there was "a general injunction of silence in the ordinary business of life, and in various ritual matters, even the bells were to remain silent", as in Catholic churches they still do, clashing out in rejoicing when Easter morning comes at last. Children were often told the bells had gone to Rome to be blessed by the Pope, and brought back with them on their return the coloured eggs that always appeared on the table or hidden away in the garden or about the house.

These of course are Christian eggs, taken over as an obvious and heaven-sent type of the resurrection; "an emblem", according to a writer in 1783, "of the rising up out of the grave, in the same manner as the chick entombed, as it were, in the egg, is in due time brought to life." The practice of taking eggs, hard-boiled and coloured scarlet or yellow, in decorated baskets to church for a blessing before or after Mass on Easter Sunday is exceedingly ancient. A special prayer is provided in the *Rituale Romanum*—"Bless, Lord, we beseech thee, this thy creature of eggs, that it may become a wholesome sustenance to thy faithful servants, eating it in thankfulness to thee, on account of the resurrection of our Lord."

Some authorities, however, discount this symbolism in favour of the more "utilitarian explanation" that "during Lent eggs were forbidden in early times as articles of diet, so when Easter came, the eggs which had accumulated . . . were specially blessed, perhaps with a view to restraining gluttony after long deprivation." Certainly six weeks' accumulation would keep better if hard-boiled; I never wondered before what they did with the food they produced in Lent and weren't permitted to eat. Moreover once they were blessed these eggs, so Brand records, "have the virtue of sanctifying the entrails of the body, and are to be the first fat or fleshy nourishment (to be taken) after the abstinence of Lent."

Our modern "chocolate eggs and such like fooleries" have been described as "a degeneration of no significance". Yet they are the direct descendants of what were once known as Pasch eggs, defined in a Latin Dictionary of 1677 as "eggs given at Easter, *Ovum paschale croceum* or *luteum*". *Croceum* indicates that they were coloured yellow with saffron obtained from the crocus plant, *Crocus sativus*; *luteum* also means saffron yellow. Commonly, however, they were known as pace-eggs, or even paste-eggs or peace-eggs.

Always hard-boiled, great skill was often used to paint and decorate and colour them. Logwood chips turned them purple, cochineal pink, coffee or onion skins brown, gorse blossom yellow and the pasque-flower itself a kind of green. More ambitiously they could be wrapped in striped or patterned ribbons and then boiled to give a rainbow effect, or names and messages written on the shells in candle grease so the dye would not take and the words show up in white. More elaborate examples might be gilded or have fine designs scratched on them with a needle. At Saint Mary Woolnoth in Lombard Street, so it is said, gilded eggs with "My Redeemer" written on them were presented to all members of the Easter congregation up to 1896.

The Opies recorded a schoolgirl from Pontypool as saying in the 1950s, "We celebrate Easter Sunday by having hard-boiled eggs dyed in different colours. We go out with our friends to a grassy hill and roll them down, and the person whose egg is the last to be broken is the winner." This egg-rolling, known in England and more particularly in Scotland, as pace-egging, is a custom of considerable antiquity; north of the Trent it persisted among children as late as 1964 and may still continue. Moreover it was frequently reported by travellers in Europe and as far away as Greece and Mesopotamia. Immigrants took it to America, where it was once practised on the lawns of the White House, but proved so bad for the grass the venue was changed to the terraces outside the Capitol itself.

Why they do it, however, the competitors don't seem to know. The Christian explanation, almost certainly *a posteriori*, is that "rolling eggs refers to the rolling away of the stone from the tomb of Christ". If this were likely, which it is not, it would scarcely account for the secondary sport of "dumping and jarping", that is knocking your egg against somebody else's to see which will break. As with conkers, the owner of an egg which cracks another "is invested with the title of 'A cock of one, two, three, etc.' ", and the last egg remaining unbroken finally wins.

Another tradition, the probable origin of later Easter bonnets and Easter parades, is that "one should wear something new on Easter Sunday, or be unlucky throughout the year". The warning was generally given in verse:

> At Easter let your clothes be new,
> Or else be sure you will it rue.

Children in Scotland used to mock at and make fun of their companions who failed to observe this rule, calling them Paseyads or Paysyads. This fascinating word is defined by Jamieson as "a contemptuous designation conferred on a female who has nothing new to appear in at Easter, originating from the custom . . . of having a new dress for the festival." Properly speaking a yad is an old mare, though here it simply implies a foolish person; pase or pays, of course, is pasch. So a paseyad is an Easter fool.

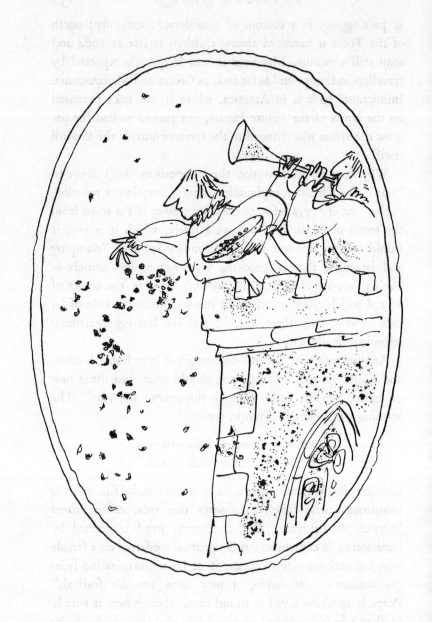

12

SUNDAY IN WHITE

For more than five hundred years the Sunday after Easter has been known in England as Low Sunday—"*Inferius Pascha*, the Lower Easter-Sunday"—and the reasons suggested for this name are many and various. Some say it was so called "because a kind of second but lower celebration of the great feast", others that it probably arose "from the contrast between the joys of Easter and the first return to ordinary Sunday services" —the dust-cart, as it were, following the Lord Mayor's Show. Or simply because it was the Sunday "below" Easter Day quite literally; that is, underneath it in the Church Calendar.

Then there are those who believe that "low" is a misunderstanding of some other word. They suggest it should really be *Laudes* Sunday, from the first word in the Sequence for the day, but this seems too remote both in sense and sound to be acceptable. Besides it already has another similar title, less common here than on the Continent—Quasimodo, from the first two words of the Introit, *Quasi modo geniti infantes*, like to new-born babes. Victor Hugo gave this name to his Hunchback who was found abandoned outside the church of Notre Dame on Low Sunday; it is also borne by the modern Sicilian poet, Salvatore Quasimodo.

What seems the most likely explanation, however, is that this was once Close Sunday, *Pascha clausum*, the Octave of Easter, the end of Easter Week. There is a parallel usage in French; Littré defines *Pâques closes* as *le dimanche de Quasimodo, qui suit celui de Pâques*. But it has other names too. In Scotland it is sometimes known as Old Men's Easter, why I do not know. And in Church Calendars, especially in early times, it often appeared as *Dominica in albis*, more properly *in albis deponendis*, the Sunday on which converts, newly baptised on Easter Day, took off and laid aside the white robes they had worn for their reception.

Commonly *Dominica in albis* became Sunday in White or White Sunday. But in England for nearly a thousand years this name has been transferred to the feast of Pentecost, seven weeks after Easter. First appearing in the eleventh century as Hwita Sunnandaeg, it has been known in one form or another as Whitsunday ever since.

The feast of Pentecost or Whitsunday commemorates for Christians the descent upon the apostles of the Holy Ghost, "the Spirit of truth, (who) will guide you into all truth", yet once again there is nothing in its name to remind us of this. The bereaved apostles were assembled together in Jerusalem because they were observing another Jewish feast. In New Testament Greek it had come to be called Pentecost, but this was not properly its name. It was intended as a thanksgiving for harvest and generally known as Hag Shabuoth, "the feast of weeks, the first-fruits of the wheat harvest".

The second day of the Passover marked the ceremonial beginning of the barley harvest. One of the first sheaves to be cut, called the Omer, was presented to the Lord as a wave-offering, according to ancient practice: "When ye be come into the land which I give unto you, and shall reap the harvest thereof, then ye shall bring a sheaf of the first-fruits of your harvest unto the priest; and he shall wave the sheaf before the Lord, to be accepted for you; on the morrow after the Sabbath the priest shall wave it." This waving or moving to and fro of an offering in front of the altar symbolized the dedication of the harvest to the Lord and his return of it to the people for their enjoyment.

A similar wave-offering was made at Hag Shabuoth, the start of the wheat harvest, this time of "the first two loaves made out of the new wheat". The date of this feast was carefully calculated—"Seven weeks shalt thou number unto thee; begin to number the seven weeks from such time as thou beginnest to put the sickle to the corn." These days were marked off one by one by the Jews both in their homes and in their synagogues; the process was known as the Counting of the Omer and the feast itself fell on the fiftieth day from the second day of the Passover, and thus the same day of the week.

In later times, when the Jews became more urbanised, the Feast of Weeks tended to lose its original significance. People looked on it merely as marking the end of Passover or as a commemoration of the giving of the Law to Moses on Mount Sinai, an event which took place, "in the third month", the month of Sivan, when the Feast of Weeks also occurred.

All this has little in common with the Christian Pentecost except the coincidence of date, and the fact that in religious mythology no correspondence is ever coincidental. According to the evangelists Christ died on the second day of the Passover, the day from which the Counting of the Omer began. Fifty days later, "when the day of Pentecost was fully come", the disciples "were all together with one accord in one place", presumably to keep the Feast. Then suddenly "there came a sound from heaven as of a rushing mighty wind . . . And there appeared unto them cloven tongues like as of fire, and it sat upon each of them. And they were all filled with the Holy Ghost, and began to speak with other tongues, as the Spirit gave them utterance."

Why Pentecost? The answer is simple. It comes from Greek *pentecostos*, meaning fiftieth; the day of Pentecost was *pentecoste hemera*, the fiftieth day. But the name, it seems, was used to refer to the whole period of Counting the Omer as much as the actual fiftieth day itself. In the Vulgate Saint Luke's phrase becomes *et cum complerentur dies Pentecostes*, translated by

Wyclif as "Whanne the dayes Pentecostes weren fulfilled", to which he adds a gloss for Pentecostes, "that is, fyfti". Early Christian writers gave this title to the whole of the Paschal season, fifty days of rejoicing and "continuous festival, during which no fast was permitted and prayer was said standing".

By the fifth century, however, Pentecost usually implies the actual day on which the Holy Ghost descended, now celebrated fifty days after Easter Sunday. Thus Aelfric, about the year 1000, writes, "Thes daegtherlica daeg (this present day, today) is ure Pentecostes, that is, se fifteoyotha daeg fram tham Easterdaeg." And Pentecost or some variant of the original Greek the feast has generally remained; in France *Pentecôte*, in Italy *Pentecoste*, in Spain *Pentecostes*, in Germany *Pfingsten*, in Denmark *Pintse*, in Holland *Pinxteren* or *Pinxter*.

Now it was the Dutch, under their famous leader Peter Stuyvesant, who settled what is now New York and called it New Amsterdam. When the English took it over and renamed it for James, Duke of York, Stuyvesant retired to his farm, the "Great Bouverie", and there died in 1672. All his life he was a man of strict morals and a rigid Sabbatarian; strange that one of his legacies to his adopted country was Pinkster, the Dutch word for Pentecost. Pinkster, now classed as "historical", seems to have been used by New Yorkers till the end of the nineteenth century. By then it signified what we should call Whit Monday and was a great holiday for the coloured people of the town. *Harper's Magazine* noted in 1881, "the Pinkster festivities commenced on Monday after Whitsunday, and now began the fun of the negroes, for Pinkster was the carnival of the African race." Or, as Bartlett put it somewhat earlier, "On Pinxter Monday the Dutch negroes . . . consider themselves especially privileged to get as drunk as they can." It is sad that by 1896 Earle could say of Pinkster Day that its name "is now almost forgotten".

But in English Pentecost, except for some fancy spelling,

remained unaltered, chiefly because it was only rarely used. In 1481 Caxton recorded "there helde they theyr penthecost or wytsontyde"; and later old Capulet, discussing with his cousin how long they were "past their dancing days", calculates:

'Tis since the nuptial of Lucentio,
Come Pentycost as quickly as it will,
Some five and twenty years; and then we mask'd.

Further references, however, are few and most of them seem chiefly technical or academic.

In spite of this it does occasionally occur as a given name for men and for women from Norman times, but never was common and almost disappeared after the Reformation. There is a record in 1201 of a certain Gaufridus *filius* Pentecostes, and as a family name it has a persistent life under such disguises as Pentercost, Pentycross, Perrycost and, rather unexpectedly, Pankhurst.

Nowadays Pentecost has something of an erudite, pedantic flavour, referring quite specifically to a feast of the Church and more common among Catholics than Anglicans, to whom that long procession of "Sundays after Trinity" are known as the "Sundays after Pentecost". Until the end of last century, however, we might have been dunned for what were called Pentecostalia or Pentecostals, offerings made by parishes to the cathedral church at Pentecost. Apparently these grew "from voluntary offerings from those who, according to custom, visited the mother church of the diocese at that season, into a fixed payment from every parish to the bishop, recoverable in the ecclesiastical court."

But their history was far less straightforward than it sounds. We hear Bishop Latimer in 1549 complaining, "I should have receyved a certayne dutye that they cal a Pentecostal", and his very way of speaking gives it an unfamiliar ring;

indeed no earlier use of the word is recorded by the *OED*. In 1797 the *Encyclopaedia Britannica* talks of "Whitsun Farthings . . . otherwise called Smoke farthings", and defines them as "a composition for offerings . . . anciently made in Whitsun-week by every man in England, who occupied a house with a chimney, to the cathedral church of the diocese."

Now before the Reformation money was certainly collected from the occupier "of each hous that smoke out of come", but this was Peter's Pence and it went to the Bishop of Rome. Henry VIII quite naturally abolished this payment, but the pennies or halfpennies or farthings were still collected. All that changed was their name and their destination. This is confirmed by the records of Holy Trinity, Minchinhampton, where in 1575 it was noted, "Expendyd at the Bishoppes vysytation to the sumner for Peter-pence or smoke farthings, some time due to the Anthecriste of roome, 10d." In parts of England, it is said, such Pentecostals were paid as late as 1895.

There is, of course, the adjective pentecostal, "of or relating to the descent of the Holy Spirit . . . like that of the day of Pentecost in Acts 2." Staid as it sounds, it has some-thing exuberant, exotic, revivalistic about it, and this is not surprising since on that day the apostles began to speak in strange languages and everyone thought they were drunk. This sense of direct inspiration was seized on by a group of evangeli-cal Christians in Los Angeles about the end of last century, men who "sought a baptism in the Holy Spirit, accompanied by speaking with tongues similar to instances recorded in Acts," and who banded together to form the first Pentecostal Church.

Their movement flourished and was brought across to England by a certain T. B. Bennett, who conducted a series of revival meetings in Sunderland in September 1907. Under his influence small groups sprang up in different places, mostly led by laymen; in 1955 there were as many as a thousand such

Pentecostal Churches, with a total membership of over fifty thousand souls. Their methods were frankly emotional, their aims "the individual attainment of holiness, perfection and a regenerative experience comparable to the Pentecostal experience of the first Christian disciples." As with most Evangelicals, their doctrines were fundamentalist; they also laid great stress on "religious excitement . . . accompanied by ecstatic utterances interpreted as the gift of tongues."

All this sounds inexpressibly remote from the English weekend popularly known as Whitsun—at least until it was transformed by Act of Parliament into the frankly pagan Spring Bank Holiday. Somehow the feast had lost its Graeco-Latin description and acquired another, which it did, according to Skeat, not long after 1066, it being "tolerably certain that the English name White Sunday is not older than the Norman Conquest, for before that time the name was always Pentecost. We are therefore quite sure that, for some reason or other, the name Pentecost was then exchanged for that of White Sunday, which came into common use."

Post hoc, in this case, however, is almost certainly not *propter hoc*, since Whitsunday, far from being French, comes from Scandinavia, paralleled by the old Norse *Hvitasunnendaeg*, Danish *Hvidessontag* and Dutch *Witten Sondagh*. A similar expression must have been current here before the Normans arrived; significantly its earliest written appearance is in an English chronicle dated about 1100: "On thisan Eastron com se kyng to Wincestre, & sona aefter tham Mathild seo hlaefdige (lady) hider to lande . . . on Hwitan Sunnandaeg."

A little later the word has become slightly Anglicised, an Old English Homily referring to "the holi goste thet thu on hwitesunedei sendest". In a second Homily of about 1175 the spelling is different again and the *h* has disappeared; we are told of the "muneyeing of tham hali gast that he sende in his apostles on thon dei that is icleped wit-sunne-dei". This

version, adopted by Wyclif as witsondai and widely used, soon
led to a popular new derivation. People, says Skeat, forgot
that the first element was *white* and wrongly supposed it to
relate to "the wit or wisdom conferred by the Holy Ghost on
the day of Pentecost, on which theme it was easy for the preacher
(to whom etymology was no object) to expatiate."

Nor were the preachers alone. According to a medieval
poet,

> This day wit-sonday is cald,
> For wisdom and wit seven fald
> Was zonen to the Apostles on this day.

Wynkyn de Worde was of the same opinion: "This day is
called Wytsonday because the Holy Ghost brought wytte and
wysdom into Christis disciples . . . and filled them full of
ghostly wytte." This wit is not of course what we usually mean
by the word—"the power of giving sudden intellectual pleasure
by unexpected combining or contrasting of previously uncon-
nected ideas or expressions." In its older sense it had the
meaning of intelligence, good judgment, even wisdom; what
the *Cursor Mundi* defines as:

> The gift o wijt o under-standing,
> O consail, strenght, o gode dreding,
> O conand-scipe, and o pite.

We still use it something in this way when we say a man
"hasn't the wit" to know or comprehend.

Though incorrect this derivation was at least an intelligent
and reasonable guess. The same can scarcely be said for those
enthusiasts who concluded that Witsuntide or Witentide "was
the time for selecting the wise men of the Witangemot",
the *Witan* being "the national council of Anglo-Saxon times"
and the *gemot* or moot its meeting.

Even allowing that the proper name of the feast is White

Sunday, and that we have preserved this, through such exotic spellings as Wijt sundai, Wissonday, Wythssonday, Qwytsonnday and even Qhythsontyd, in our modern Whit Sunday, there is still another misunderstanding to be cleared away. For it seems that at one time in some parts of England, notably Worcestershire, Shropshire, Warwickshire, Leicestershire and Hampshire, "farmers . . . used to give all the milk of their cows to all their neighbours who chose to go for it on Whit Sunday morning." From this apparently inexplicable access of charity, this habit "of the rich giving all the milk of their cows to the poor", the day is said to have taken its name, for the plain reason that milk is proverbially white.

Then again John Squire, Vicar of Saint Leonard's, Shoreditch, in the early seventeenth century records that it was also the custom for white bread to be given as a dole to the poor on this Sunday. In a notable Whitsuntide sermon he made the best of all worlds, insisting that "the day was so named on four grounds", which he lists as follows. First, from the time of the year—"*tempus albi solus*, when the season was attended by the greatest sunshine". Second, from the custom of the day—"this was *Dominica in Albis*; they used *albis vestibus post baptismum*". Third, from the mercy of God to man, which was shown "by the Holy Ghost coming down to man on this day". Fourth, from the mercy of man to man, shown "by the gift of white loaves to the poor".

Of Squire's four reasons the second is the true one. This Sunday was certainly named from the *albati* or newly baptized, who wore white robes for the ceremony and for some while after. Yet it is fire we associate with Pentecost, not water. The liturgical colour for the day, as for all Masses of the Holy Ghost, is red. At one time red rose leaves used to drift down from church roofs in token of the "cloven tongues like as of fire", and in parts of France trumpets were blown "to represent the sound of the mighty wind which accompanied the descent of the Holy Ghost". Baptism seems irrelevant, yet its association with Whitsunday is very ancient.

For baptism in the early Church was not simply sprinkling a child's head three times with water *in nomine Patris et Filii et Spiritus Sancti*, and giving it a name. What was needed was faith and infants cannot reason, hence the long debate, still continuing, as to whether they should be baptized. For an adult, however, the process could be very easy. Saint Philip, thumbing a lift in the chariot of the Ethiopian eunuch, treasurer to Queen Candace, had expounded to him only one text when "they came unto a certain water; and the eunuch said, See, here is water; what doth hinder me to be baptized? And Philip said, If thou believest with all thine heart, thou mayest . . . And they went down both into the water . . . and he baptized him." For baptize is simply the Greek word *baptizein*, to bathe, from *baptein*, to dip.

But as the Church grew and expanded more was demanded of its converts than a mere expression of belief. Sacramental baptism became a ceremony, the culmination of a long period of teaching and preparation. On the eve of the appointed day the candidates (which word itself means "clothed in white", from *candidus*) were expected to fast and keep vigil. Then, in their white robes, they made confession of their sins, renounced the devil, and were baptized either by triple immersion or by "standing semi-immersed in water, up to the knees or waist, combined with three-fold pouring over the head." Fonts were much larger in those days; huge basins such as still can be seen in Ravenna, Florence and Siena. They were housed in a separate building, known as a baptistery, usually octagonal or round, and here all the converts and later all the babies of the city would come to be made members of the Church.

Nor could you be baptized just whenever you chose; the proper time was Easter. During the Easter liturgy water and oil were, and still are, hallowed and the font was blessed; then came the baptisms, for which the rubrics still allow. But when Christianity spread to northern Europe, to Scandinavia and Britain, perhaps, as Vigfusson suggests, "owing to the cold weather at Eastertime, Pentecost, as the birthday of the Church, seems to have been especially appointed for christening and for ordination." Hence *Dominica in Albis* or White Sunday.

When infant baptism, owing to the general belief that unbaptized children who died were barred from heaven, became usual practice the adult candidates in their white robes were forgotten. So a later authority, attempting to account for Whitsunday, says it comes from "the white coifs worn by the babies baptized at that time". This "white cloth set by the minister at baptism upon the head of the newly anointed with chrism", a mixture of oil and balm symbolizing the gift of the Holy Spirit, was known as a chrism cloth or chrisom. The child thus baptized was called a chrisom child, and if it should die within the month it was shrouded in the chrisom cloth, perhaps as its passport to heaven. Hence Mistress Quickly's comment on Falstaff's death: "A' made a finer end and went away an it had been any christom child," a comparison so strange as to be infinitely touching.

There may indeed be some truth in this suggestion, for a homilist whom I cannot date wrote, according to Brand, "In the begynnyng of holi chirch, all the children weren kept to be crystened on thys even, at the font hallowyng (that is, Whitsun Eve); but now, for enchesone[1] in so long abydynge they might dye without crystendome, therefore holi chirch ordeyneth to crysten at all times of the yeare; save eyght dayes before these evenys (Easter and Whitsunday), the childe shalle abyde till the font hallowyng, if it may savely for perill of death, and ells not."

Whitsunday, depending on the date of Easter, is a movable feast and may fall in either May or June. In Scotland, however,

[1] *occasionem*, for the reason that.

Whitsunday need have no connexion with the Sabbath. For as well as a Church festival it is also a term-day, that is, "under Scots law the usual day for the removal of tenants of both burgh and rural tenements", and also the day on which servants or labourers engaged by the year or half-year took up their positions.

The confusion that might arise from a movable quarter-day is obvious. A hypothetical Whitsunday was therefore appointed, to fall upon May 15. An Act of William and Mary dated 1693 proclaims that "Our Soveraigne Lord and Lady the King and Queen's Majesties . . . Declare that the Fifteenth Day of May was since the date of the forsaid Act, and shall be in all time comeing in place of the former Terme of Whitsunday, to all effects whatever."

On this day, even as late as the end of the nineteenth century, there was great bustle everywhere, especially in "the towns of Scotland, which present an animated appearance from the number of removals or changes of residence; the streets are crowded with household goods being removed from one house to another." And though the Act proclaimed that May 15 should stand "in place of the former Terme of Whitsunday", it still kept its old name. This must surely be the only instance of a Sunday in the middle of the week.

13

DAUNSYNGES, DRUNKENNESS AND WHOREDOME

If a child was born at Pentecost, Pentecost it might be christened, never Whitsun. True it seems to occur as a surname, with the spelling Hwyttesone or Whitsone, from as early as the fourteenth century. Here appearance is deceptive, for it has no relation to the feast; it either means "son of White or Whitt" or is "a simplified pronunciation of Whitston, white stone", as in Whitson or White Stone Farm.

The reason for this strange omission lies deep in the history of the word. White Sunday became Whitsunday, the first syllable was shortened, people forgot its original significance and soon began to divide it not as Whit-Sunday but as Whitsun-Day. From this by the thirteenth century came Whitesune-tide, or Whitsun-tide, which either describes "the time of the white sun"[1] or is meaningless, yet everyone knew what it meant. For Whitsun, like Christmas and Easter, had become an adjective denoting "something belonging to, connected with or occurring at the season of Whitsunday".

The next obvious step, to drop the ending and to speak of Whitsun-tide as Whitsun, as we habitually do, was very long delayed. The *OED* at the beginning of the twentieth century still recorded this use as "rare"; its first quotation is from Disraeli and dated 1849. Since then the practice has become so common it never occurs to us to question it. We might quite happily give Whitsun as a font-name if we felt so

[1] And so interpreted by the Rev. John Squire in his translation *tempus albi solus*—see p. 147 above.

inclined. But our ancestors could not, since for them no such name existed, even for the feast.

With the adjective, however, they were very familiar. For them a feast was a feast, and this one they kept with eating and drinking, dancing, sports and games. In fact they held a Whitsun Ale.

Brewer, in his charmingly dated explanation, says "the word *ale* is used in such composite words as church-ale, Whitsun-ale, etc., for revel or feast, ale being the chief liquor given. We talk now in the same way of giving 'a tea', and at the 'Varsity, 'Will you wine with me after hall?' means, 'Will you come to my rooms for dessert—wine, fruit and cigars, with coffee to follow?' " Strange that we still give "a tea" but not yet "a coffee"; perhaps in time it may come.

An Ale then could commonly mean "a festival or merry-making at which much ale is drunk, an ale-drinking". Some indeed have maintained the word ale is a form of yule and meant a feast or festival, the beverage taking its name from the celebration rather than *vice versa*. This, however, begs many questions about the significance of yule. All we can be certain of is that ale or *ealu*, from Old Norse *öl*, properly describes what the *OED* calls "intoxicating liquor made from an infusion of malt by fermentation". Its earlier history is uncertain, though it may be related to Latin *alumen*, alum, "whence astringent or bitter", the equivalent perhaps of "A pint of bitter, please."

But bitter, strictly speaking, is not ale, it is beer. The distinction is a fine one and often no attempt was made to draw it. The same liquor, wrote a tenth century poet, "is called ale among men, and among the gods beer". Beer, the Old English *beor* and the German *bier*, once meant merely a drink and is obscurely related to Latin *bibere*. We English, it seems, are the only people to retain both ale and beer in our language; Scandinavians have ale, and Germans beer.

This beer by definition is ale fortified by the addition of "the wicked weed called Hops".

> When I was a brewer longe,
> With hoppes I made my ale stronge,

says a character in one of the sixteenth century Chester Plays. And a recipe of 1502 for making "lx barellis of sengyll beer" specifies "X quarters malte, ij quarters wheet, ij quarters ootes, xl ll'weight of hoppys".

These same "hoppys", still widely grown in Kent and Sussex, were first introduced into the south of England about the year 1524. They probably came from Flanders, and this in itself would account for the revival of the old name beer. One disapproving writer complained in 1542 that "bere is made of malte, of hoppes and water: it is a naturell drynke for a Dutche man. And nowe of late dayes it is moche used in Englande, to the detryment of many Englysshe men."

Life was changing in other ways about this time. Even the date became proverbial; in 1524 "it happened that divers things were newly brought into England, whereupon this Rhyme was made:

> Turkeys, Carps, Hoppes, Piccarell and Beer,
> Came into England all in one year."

Or, as another version has it, "Peacocks, Hops and Heresie came first into England in one and the same ship." A little early, one might think, for turkeys, and for peacocks a little late; Chaucer had written of "the pecok, with his aungels fethres brighte". Yet turkeys, it seems, did appear in England during the sixteenth century; this name was given to what we now call the guinea-fowl, "probably because it was originally brought from New Guinea by the Portuguese through Turkish dominions." Carp and pickerel, or young pike, had for long stocked monkish fish-ponds, and heresy was surely endemic long before Henry VIII. But there does seem little doubt about the hops.

Ale has always been considered as *par excellence* the Englishman's drink, the wine of England. And the habits of those who enjoy it have changed very little. Caxton, noting in 1480 that

> When they drinke atte ale
> They telle many a lewd tale,

might have been writing of almost any men in almost any pub. Another author, a little later, observed of the English workmen, in this case carpenters:

> When thei have wrought an oure or two,
> Anone to the ale thei wylle go.

And in the eighteenth century, the days of empire building, it was proverbially said that "in settling an island, the first building erected by a Spaniard will be a church; by a Frenchman, a fort; by a Dutchman, a warehouse; by an Englishman, an ale-house."

What better way, then, to celebrate Whitsuntide or any other feast than by drinking ale? The habit moreover is longstanding, inherited from our Norse ancestors; in pagan times an integral part of Scandinavian festivals was ale "brewed in vats so large that Saxo Grammaticus declares a Danish prince, Hundrig, was accidentally drowned in one". Missionaries sent to convert these ignorant heathen are said to have found a group of men "sitting round an enormous vat of ale" who "described themselves as worshipping Wotan". To this pleasant religious observance the missionaries themselves appear to have been converted, for at one time Norwegian law enjoined "the brewing of ale before all Christian festivals, and its consumption in the company of neighbours, under penalty of a fine."

In England somewhat similar drinking parties, known as Ales, were centred on the churches. Organised by the whole parish, they were in some ways the forerunners of our garden fêtes, bazaars or coffee mornings; everyone enjoyed themselves and at the same time contributed towards the church funds or other good cause.

Indeed what was called a Church Ale seems often to have been organised expressly to raise money. The disapproving Stubbes recorded in 1583 the mechanics of such an affair, making it sound irresistibly like a modern Bring and Buy, only rather less sedate. "In certain towns, where dronken Bacchus beares swaie . . . the church-wardens of every parishe, with the consent of the whole parishe, provide halfe a score or twentie quarters of maulte, whereof some they buy of the church stocke, and some is given to them of the parishioners themselves, every one conferring somewhat, according to his abilitie; which maulte being made into very strong ale or beer, is sette to sale, either in the church or some other place, assigned to this purpose. Then when this is set abroache, well is he that can gete the soonest to it, and spend the most at it . . . That money, they say, is to repaire their churches and chappels with, to buy bookes for service, cuppes for the celebration of the Sacrament, surplesses for Sir John, and such other necessaries." Sir John here, of course, is a generic name for the parson, his title of "Sir" being the equivalent of Latin *Dominus*, as in Italy the priest is still called Don Giovanni or Don Camillo.

An excuse, in fact, is never lacking for the holding of an Ale; there were Mary Ales, Lamb Ales, Help Ales, "Soule Ales, called also Dirge Ales", Bed Ales, Clerk Ales, Leet Ales, Scot Ales and Bride Ales. A Mary Ale took place on a feast-day of the Blessed Virgin, Candlemas perhaps or the Annunciation. A Lamb Ale was given by a farmer when his lambing season was over or at the time of the lamb-shearing. A Help Ale was a kind of harvest festival, held to celebrate the completion of some communal piece of work such as hay-making or cutting the corn, in the days when men gave their help to their neighbour in return for his when they themselves were busy.

Soul Ales or Dirge Ales explain themselves. They accompanied requiems and funerals, and were probably no more occasions of rejoicing than the funeral feast has ever been. This dirge, incidentally, which now means "a song sung at a burial, or in commemoration of the dead", when it doesn't merely stand for something inexpressibly dreary, was once the name given to the Office of Matins for the Dead, chanted by monks on appropriate occasions. It is no more than a corruption of the first word of the constantly repeated antiphon to the first psalm: *Dirige, Domine, Deus meus, in conspectu tuo viam meam*, direct, O Lord my God, my way in thy sight. Often it was corrupted still further, as a traveller in 1730 remarked at a Scottish funeral: "Wine is filled about as fast as it can go round, till there is hardly a sober person among them . . . This last homage they call the Drudgy (or Dredgy), but I suppose they mean the Dirge, that is, a service performed for a dead person."

Another somewhat similar ceremony, said to have survived in northern England until the end of last century, was Arval or Arvel. This, from *arfr-öl*, was also a funeral feast, with this distinction, that the meaning of *arfr* is "inheritance"; the holding of an Arvel or Inheritance Ale meant the dead man had property to leave. This is clear from a definition of 1780: "On the decease of any person possessed of valuable effects, the friends and neighbours of the Family are invited to dinner on the day of Interment, which is called the Arthel or Arvel-dinner." The food offered to the guests at one such "arvill or treat" is recorded as "cold posset, stewed prunes, cake and cheese". Not much of a treat, we might think.

Complementing the Soul Ale was the Bed Ale, rather less

exciting than it sounds, for its other name was Groaning Ale. When a woman bore a child it used to be said she was "brought to bed of a son", and after the event friends and relatives would call to share her happiness and to celebrate the birth. They might perhaps assemble round the bed, but more commonly the mother was made comfortable in a groaning chair, "a rustic name for a chair in which a woman sits after her confinement to receive congratulations". Those who called were naturally offered the appropriate refreshment—groaning cake, groaning cheese and groaning malt or ale, brewed especially strong for the occasion.

The groaning, of course, applies to the actual birth; in 1579 North wrote of Ariadne, "when her groning time was come . . . she died in labour." This too is Hamlet's allusion; Ophelia tells him, "You are keen, sir, you are keen", and he replies, "It would cost you a groaning to take off my edge." Since children were often baptized very shortly after birth the Bed Ale or Groaning Ale might also embrace the christening. That famous school Bedales, however, is no relation; it is merely one of the many variant spellings of the surname Beadle.

As for Clerk Ales, these it seems were a kind of benefit for the poor Parish Clerk. Leet Ales took place when the Lord of the Manor held the yearly Leet or Manor Court, dealing with local disputes and petty offences. A Scot Ale was probably "a festival at which ale was drunk at the invitation of the Lord of the Manor" or of one of his employees such as the forester or bailiff, for which Ale a forced contribution was levied. Hence the name "Scot", meaning a payment or a fine. It sounds very like a Dutch treat, but "the nature of this exaction is very obscure". Another definition, given in 1598, is plain enough, however: "A Scottall or Scot-ale is, where any officer of the Forest doth keepe an Alehouse and by colour of his office doth cause men to come to his house, and there to spend their money for fear of having his displeasure." In other words, buy my beer or it will be the worse for you.

Bride Ales, of course, we still hold, though we expect our glasses filled with champagne, not the "warmed, sweetened and spiced ale presented to a wedding party on its return from Church", which is what the word still meant in Yorkshire in the nineteenth century. Back in Anglo-Saxon times the *brydealu* or bride-ale was specifically and exclusively the wedding banquet or feast, later known as the wedding breakfast—and "break fast" it literally was in the days when to take communion one had to have fasted since midnight. But when Wyclif points out in his commentary on the *Song of Solomon* that it concerns "the bridalis of Crist and of the Chirche" the word carries all the implications of a wedding or marriage today.

As a noun it was, like espousals, often plural; by Shakespeare's time it had become in the singular a common adjective. So Katharine in *The Taming of the Shrew* bids the company, "Gentlemen, forward to the bridall dinner". Bride ale has contracted to bridal, and a bridal dinner is simply a wedding feast. However because the word sounded as if it should really mean "of or pertaining to a bride, worn by a bride", it was habitually used with this sense. Strictly speaking the phrase "a bridal gown" is ambiguous; it may mean a wedding dress, it may mean a gown that is worn by a bride.

Now this bride is very ancient and nobody knows what it means. Skeat suggests it derives from an Old Teutonic word for promised or bespoke—one engaged to be married, in fact— while the *OED* thinks it may be a Teutonic name for a daughter-in-law, from the root *bru-*, to cook, brew, make broth, these being "the duty of a daughter-in-law in the primitive family". Certainly the bride was so important that even the groom was named after her. He was called the *brydguma* or bridegome, *guma* being the equivalent of Latin *homo*, man; therefore the bride's man. In time *gome* became confused with groom, which once meant a boy or a man before it was narrowed down to a man-servant, with "the special sense of horse-attendant"; hence our modern bridegroom. Even the wedding-guests used to be known as bridallers; a pity we lost that very pleasant expression.

Most of these Ales were of a family or private nature; Whitsun Ales, with their sport and feasting, dancing and games, were for everyone to enjoy. This tradition, "in the which with leappynge, daunsynge and kyssynge they mayntayne the profett of their churche", together with the season of the year, probably led to our own fixed conviction that Whit-Monday is a time for pleasure; sports, fairs, games and church fêtes. Of this the Puritan minded have always disapproved; one Harrison in 1587 commented on "the heathenish rioting at bride-ales", and a certain Parson Kethe about the same time deplored the practice of holding Ales on a Sunday, "which day is spent in bulbeatings, bearebeatings, bowlings, dicyng, cardyng, daunsynges, drunkenness and whoredome, in so much as men could not keepe their servaunts from lyinge out of theyr owne houses that same Sabbath-day at night."

Ordinary people, however, shared the opinion of the poet who believed that age to be happy

> When every village did a May-pole raise,
> And Whitsun-Ales and May-games did abound.

Against the opposition of the spoil-sports Charles I even went so far as to issue an official Act providing "that after the end of Divine Service, Our good people be not disturbed, letted, or discouraged from . . . having of May-games, Whitson-Ales and Morris Dances." About the Continental Sunday, it seems, there is nothing very new.

Much effort and organization went into the Whitsun Ales. Committees, of course, were elected and two parishioners chosen to take charge and preside at the feast. Often these were called the Lord and Lady of the Ale, or the Whitsun-lord and Whitsun-lady. Sometimes they were both men, and had other more fanciful names; the parish records of Mere in Wiltshire tell how "John Watts, the sonne of Thomas Watts, is appointed to be Cuckowe King this next year, because he was Prince last year; And Thomas Barnard the younger is elected Prince for this next year."

Once appointed, the first job of the organisers was to make a general collection, and to bestow it "in brewing, baking and other acates, against Whitsontide". When the day arrived all the villagers met at the church or on the green, each bringing food or drink of his own as well as what was provided, "contributing some petty portion to the stock, which, by many smalls, groweth to a meetly greatness." Charges were made for the ale, for the cakes, and perhaps for competing in the games, "and in this way (they) frankly spend their money together. The afternoons are consumed in such exercises as olde and yong folke (having leisure) do accustomably weare out the time withall . . . When the feast is ended, such money as exceedeth the disbursement is layd up in store, to defray any extraordinary charges arising in the parish." The Mere churchwardens' accounts record for three successive years profits from the Whitsun Ale of £15, £20 and £23, in the sixteenth century quite respectable sums.

John Aubrey some hundred years later maintained that these despised merrymakings collected more money to support the poor of the parish than the recently established Poor Law Authorities. "There were no rates for the poor in my grandfather's day," he wrote; "the Church-Ale of Whitsuntide did the business. In every parish is (or was) a church-house to which belonged spits, crocks etc., utensils for dressing provision. Here the house-keepers met and were merry and gave their charity. The young people had dancing, bowling, shooting at butts, etc., the ancients sitting gravely by and looking on. All things were civil and without scandal"—a typical English garden party, in fact.

"The Church-Ale", Aubrey concludes, "is doubtless derived from the *Agapai* or Love Feasts, mentioned in the New Testament." Insofar as it appears that at the Love Feasts, held by early Christians before or after communion, "wealthy or well-to-do Christians brought the materials of the feast, in which the poorer brethren who had nothing to bring shared equally," and sometimes collections were made for the poor, he may be right. But his wicket is a little sticky, for Saint Paul himself soon fell to denouncing these communal meals where "one is hungry and another is drunken", asking the loving feasters, "What, have ye not houses to eat and drink in?" By the time of the Council of Carthage in 397 they had become such a scandal they were condemned.

In old parish accounts for Whitsun-Ales such odd entries sometimes appear as, "For making a new pair of pigeing-holes, 2s 6d", or "Good wife Ansell for the pigeon-holes, 1s 6d." Naively I thought a pigeon was a dove and the dove was the Holy Spirit; there must be some connexion with the live or mechanical doves that flew symbolically down on congregations at Whitsun and often at Easter in Catholic churches:

On Whitsunday whyte pigeons tame in strings from heaven flie,
And one that framèd is of wood still hangeth in the skie.

But I was being far too clever. "Pigeon-holes" turned out to be a game "like our modern Bagatelle, where there was a machine with arches for the balls to run through, resembling the cavities made for pigeons in a dove-house." The same game, if not under the same name, is perennially resurrected at fêtes and fairs. "*Imprimis*, cleared by the pigeon holes, £4 19s od", was carefully recorded for the Brentford Whitsun Ale in 1624—a tidy profit on a probable outlay of two and six or even five bob.

14
HOGMANAY TROLOLAY

"The cry of Hogmanay Trololay is of usage immemorial in this country", asserted an anonymous contributor to the *Caledonian Magazine* in 1792. Most Scotsmen, if asked for the origins of Hogmanay, would probably say it goes back to pagan times. Pagan it certainly is and always has been. Though Watch Night services are held in many churches on New Year's Eve the custom is new, corresponding to no Christian feast unless it be the Eve of the Circumcision. Neither English nor Christian, it really has no place in this book. Yet its name and the complicated knots etymologists have tied themselves into trying to explain it are so fascinating I could not bear to leave it out.

What precisely does Hogmanay mean? No one in fact really knows. What then do we mean when we use it? Jamieson in his great *Dictionary of the Scottish Language* defines it first of all as "the name appropriated by the vulgar to the last day of the year", and we, being vulgar, would agree. It has, however, several other meanings, roughly corresponding with handsel. In some parts of Scotland and the north of England, for instance, "it was customary for everybody to make and receive presents amongst their friends on the eve of the new year, which present was called an Hagmenay." Ignore the spelling; it comes in many varieties. Sufficient that the word could mean "a New Year's gift . . . or a gratuity to tradesmen and employees on that day."

As on all such occasions "it is ordinary among some plebians in the South of Scotland to go about from door to door on New Year's Eve, crying Hagmane" and soliciting for gifts, in this case chiefly of money or of "oat cakes, bread or the like". At one time the poor made these rounds; later the children took over with their traditional song:

> Hogmanay, Trololay,
> Give us of your white bread and none of your grey.

Or in a Glasgow version:

> Hogmenay, Troll-ol, troll-oll aye,
> Gie us a piece o' your white bread
> And eke a bittock o' your grey,
> Wi' brown laif dawds, for Hogmenay.

What they received was usually an oat cake or biscuit specially baked. Kindly souls made a batch of these "biscuits" to distribute on "Cake-day", as it was sometimes known. So Hogmanay is also defined as "the gift of an oatmeal cake, or the like, which children expect, and in some parts systematically solicit, on that day; also the word shouted by children calling at friends' houses and soliciting this customary gift." Another name for this "cake of oatmeal, called a hogmoney", was a noor-cake. Strange as it sounds, its origin is simple; it is merely a slipshod version of a New Year Cake.

A more elaborate rhyme, still current among Scottish children, runs:

> Rise up, guidwife, and shake your feathers,
> Dinna think that we are beggars,
> We're girls and boys come out today
> For to get our Hogmanay.

Sometimes they even made for themselves aprons with large pockets for carrying the "noor-cakes" they collected. And if neighbours proved ungenerous they transferred their attentions to the bakers' shops. In Saint Andrews at least not so long ago "nearly every child in the town rose early on Hogmanay and made a round of the shops chanting the song:

> My feet's cauld; my shune's thin;
> Gie's my cakes and let me rin."

Only the hard-hearted could resist such a sad, disillusioned refrain.

But what about the whisky, Sassenachs will be asking? Take heart, for Hogmanay has still another meaning, this time "the entertainment given to a visitor" on New Year's Eve, which entertainment consisted chiefly of "wine and cakes, or whisky, buns and shortbread, or cheese and bread." There was also the famous "hot pint", which everyone present would "drink to each other's prosperity" and which was concocted of "a mixture of spiced and sweetened ale with an infusion of whisky".

Visitors known and unknown were welcome at Hogmanay, even though they weren't exactly Scotland's ideal "first-footer", a tall dark-haired strange man with a piece of coal in one hand and a sprig of mistletoe in the other. At any large house they would be offered a drink, bread and cheese, and shortbread or oatcakes. Not everywhere, however, would they also get a shilling, like the "too poor women" a benevolent Scotsman noted in 1696 that he "brought up to my chamber yesterday to heare them sing a hag ma nae song."

All this brings us nowhere nearer discovering the origin of this fascinating word. On balance it might be expected that its source is very ancient, Celtic perhaps or Scandinavian. Both the name and the custom were "supposed by some to be prior to the Christian faith", and on this assumption many fantastic etymologies have been constructed. They are worth recording for their ingenuity alone.

First of all, the spelling is no guide. It was passed from mouth to mouth by largely illiterate people, and written down phonetically when it was written at all, so no spelling can be said to be the true one. Calder therefore was misled when in 1694 he decided the Northumbrian version Hagmana or Hagmene was no more than "a corrupted word from the Greek *Hagia-mana*, which signifies the holy month". Alas, what he doesn't explain is why Northumbrians should start talking Greek.

More plausible is Brewer's suggestion, that "holy month" was the meaning and that its origin was Saxon, *halig-monath*. Bede in his calendar does list a *Haleg monath*, but this is the ninth month and therefore apparently September. December to him was *se aerra geola*, the former Yule, or "yoless moneth". True, among the Franks in the time of Charlemagne December was called *Heilagmanoth*. But even supposing the connexion were proved, it seems a little aberrant to go round wishing your neighbours a holy month when it is already over.

Others have attempted to relate it to Scandinavian *hoegtid*, "a term applied to Christmas and various other festivals of the Church". As *högtid* this word is good Swedish for a feast or a festival—a "high time" in fact—but its only connexion with Hogmanay is two or three letters in common.

The same may be said of the efforts to link it with *Hoggu-nott* or *Hogenat*, the name of "the night preceding Yule". *Höggva* in Icelandic meant to kill, slaughter, put to death; *Hoggu-nott* therefore means "slaughter night", so called from "the great multitude of cattle, which were sacrificed on that night, or slaughtered in preparation for the feast of the following day". Brewer, accepting this derivation, tells us "King Haco of Norway fixed the feast of Yole on Christmas Day, the eve of which used to be called hoggnight, but the Scots were taught by the French to transfer the feast of Yole to the feast of Noel, and hoggnight has ever since been the last of December." I suppose this meant something to Brewer; it confounds confusion for me.

Another bright soul had the theory that Hogmanay comes in some way from Anglo-Saxon "*hogen-hyne*, one's own domestic servant". But why on earth should it? Especially as on inquiry *hogen-hyne* or *hoghenhine* turns out to be a "barbarous form handed down in the Law books of early Middle English *ogen hine*, own domestic, member of one's own family", and that chiefly it refers to the legal status of a guest. In the days when inns were fewer and hospitality freer, people often gave beds to strangers as well as to friends. For two nights the host had no responsibility for them, but if they stayed for three they were reckoned as his "own hine" or hinds; members, that is, of his household. Or, as the lawyers put it in 1607, "*Hogenhine*, is he that commeth guest-wise to a house, and lieth there the third night. After which time he is accounted of his familie in whose house he lieth . . . and if he offend the King's Peace his Oast must be answerable for him."

From guests to feasting. One Sibb put forward an old Teutonic "*met heughe ende meugh eten*, to eat with pleasure and appetite". Pretty remote both in sound and meaning, surely?

Then some say one of the cups often drunk at the Yule feast was called Minne, "in honour of deceased relations who had acquired renown", for *minne* "simply denotes remembrance". And though in Germany, where the *Minnesinger* sang his *Minnelied*, *Minne* is love, in Old Norse it meant memory, memorial. Minnyng or Myndyng Days were those for remembering the dead; a Month's Mind was a Mass said for a relative four weeks after his death. On this basis, plus the further assumption that "our Gothic ancestors worshipped the Sun under the name of Thor, and gave the name *Oel* (or Ale) to any feast," it is only a short step to concluding that the cry of Hogmanay Trololay should quite simply be "viewed as a call to the celebration of the festival of their great god: *Hogg minne! Thor oel! oel!*", which being interpreted is "Remember your sacrifices; The Feast of Thor! The Feast!"

Hiding in the shadows, however, is a strange character called Ogmos or Ogma who according to Irish legend invented the Ogam, that esoteric Celtic alphabet providing "signs for secret speech known only to the learned". Secret they certainly were, the letters consisting of "thin lines or strokes drawn alongside or across a continuous medial or guiding line, usually the edge of a squared stone". For this reason its name may derive from Greek *ogmos*, a furrow. All the same the belief that Hercules invented it dies hard. Lucian, travelling in Gaul, reported that "he saw Hercules represented as a little old man, whom in the language of the country they called Ogmius or Ogmion. He was informed by a learned Druid that Hercules did not, in Gaul, as in Greece, betoken strength of body, but the force of eloquence", hence his connexion with the alphabet. On this Charles Mackay comments, "If Ogmus or Ogmion, the Celtic Hercules, were worshipped on the last day of the old and the beginning of the new year by the Ancient Druids, it is possible that a clue might be found to the etymology of this much disputed word." But it is a very large "if".

Mackay, who was a stern advocate of what Weekley calls "the Celtomaniac heresy" and wrote his *Gaelic Etymology* to prove English grew from Celtic roots, has his own theory. Citing Halliwell, who records Hogminnie as "a word of contempt for a young woman in Devonshire", he points out that Hogmanay is clearly related to this and comes from "Gaelic *Og*, young; *maighdean*, a maid or a virgin; *mnai*, women; whence *og-mnai* (*og-menai*), the festival of the young women." Since this sounds highly irrelevant, especially as women first-footers are definitely discouraged, I have to tell you he cheats. For he defines Hogmanay as an occasion "of the bestowal of gifts, especially to women, whether mothers, wives, sisters, sweethearts or particular friends." I hope all the good Scots ladies are fully aware of this.

Another man who twisted the word to his own uses was John Dixon, Scottish divine. Holding forth from his pulpit at Kelso against the heathen and ungodly custom of "going from door to door upon New Year's Eve crying Hagmena", he asked his congregation, "Sirs, do you know what Hagmene signifies? It is, the Devil be in the house! That's the meaning of its Hebrew original." A clear case of a preacher for whom, as Skeat remarked, "etymology was no object".

Meanwhile in Yorkshire they were quite sure the old cry was "Hagman Heigh", and the meaning plain Anglo-Saxon. A hagman is a man who hags or hacks, "one who gains his sustenance by cutting and selling wood". And Hagman-heigh was "a local New Year's custom, of demanding a Christmas box; formerly on behalf of the hagman, or woodcutter, in consideration of an extra supply of fuel at Christmas." As they went on their rounds these itinerant woodmen chanted an old song with the refrain:

> Tonight it is the New Year's night, tomorrow is the day,
> And we are come for our right and for our ray,
> As we used to do in Old King Henry's day:
> Sing fellows, sing, Hagman-heigh!

Here several wires are clearly badly crossed, and a new interpretation made simply from the sound of the word.

There seems to have been only one solitary attempt to give Hogmanay a Christian origin. This turns to that eminently Christian language French, supposing it "alludes to the time when our Saviour was born . . . (and) immediately respects the arrival of the Wise Men from the East." Hogmanay Trololay is French after the Scottish equivalent of Stratford atte Bowe, and should read:

> *Homme est né,*
> *Trois rois allois.*

That is, "a man is born, three kings are come". Or, in an alternative version,

Homme est né,
Trois rois là.

—"three kings are there". No modern etymologist has any support for this theory. Yet there is a Gaelic New Year song beginning "Three men tonight, As on Easter night——" After that, however, it merely "becomes unintelligible".

In December 1967 the *Radio Times* joined the fray with a contribution by an unnamed "correspondent from Scotland, versed in folk lore north of the Border". For him the words are Anglo-Saxon, to be understood as:

Hogmen aye,
Trolle on lay.

This does not mean, as you might imagine, that the keepers of pigs are always singing a song. No translation is given, but the explanation implies that the Hogmen always wander about (trolle) on the fields or untilled ground (lay, lea). For, says the note, "the Hogmen were the men from the hills"— the high men, presumably, as in *högtid*—"and came down from the dwellings of the Good Folk. At midnight on Hogmanay came the magic moment when the Good Folk and the Bad Folk changed their residences for the following year." It is hard to know whether this is a serious suggestion or not. It is certainly a fine example of the danger of a little knowledge and the irresponsible way many writers treat words, their stock in trade.

What then, you will be saying, is the true history of Hogmanay? Patience, we are getting warmer. Let us return to the eighteenth century gentleman and his contribution to the *Caledonian Magazine*. He too takes us back to the Druids, about whom, he says, it is well known that they "went into the woods with great solemnity on the last night of the year, where they cut the mistletoe of the oak with a golden bill, and brought it into the town and country houses . . . when it was distributed to the people to preserve them from all harms." Well, according to some it was at the summer and winter solstice, and to others "on the sixth night of the moon", but since Caesar and Pliny both record it, there seems little doubt that at some time the Druids did "cut the oak mistletoe with a golden sickle", catch it in a white cloth to stop it touching the ground, and distribute it among the worshippers as a holy charm.

Thus, continues the writer, "when Christianity was introduced among the barbarian Celts and Gauls it is probable that the clergy, when they could not completely abolish the pagan rites, would endeavour to give them a Christian turn." Fair enough. But the well-meaning priests, it seems, soon lost control of their flocks. For in France by the eighteenth century "great excesses were committed on the last night of the year . . . by companies of both sexes, dressed in fantastic habits, who ran about with their Christmas boxes, called Tire Lire, begging both money and wassail. These beggars were called Bachelettes, Guisards; and their chief Rollet Follet. They came into churches, during the service of the vigils, and disturbed the devotions by their cries of:

Au gui menez, Rollet Follet,
Au gui menez, tiri liri,
Mainte du blanc et point du bis."

As the author points out, "the resemblance of the above cry to our Hogmanay, Trololay, Give us your white bread and none of your grey; and the name Guisards given to our Bacchanals are remarkable circumstances." Indeed one begins to feel he is on to something.

But first a bit of explanation. Rollet Follet, he imagines, may have got his name from "a corruption of the ancient

Norman invocation to their hero Rollo", or more properly
Hrolfr. Hrolfr was a Norseman who conquered north-west
France, settled in the district of Rouen in 911, had himself
baptized Robert, called his country Normandy and became its
first Duke. *Tiri liri*, of course, may refer to the Christmas
boxes or more probably is just a jolly noise, from which in
fact they took their name. *Blanc* is white bread and *bis* or
pain bis is wholemeal, the word meaning greyish-brown or
brownish-grey.

As for the names of the beggars, these are not supported by
Littré. He defines a *bachelette* as *une jeune fille gracieuse*, and
thinks the word once meant a servant—though of course a
servant might well be looking for a Christmas box. The only
Guisards he lists are the followers of the Duc de Guise during
the Wars of Religion. Yet the word is undoubtedly French
and was used in Scotland to describe what we would call
Mummers, men "dressed in fantastic habits" who went from
house to house acting, dancing and singing at the season of
Hogmanay.

And what of the essential phrase *Au gui menez*? This is
sometimes written *Au gueux menez*, and said to mean "Bring
to the beggars", give us money and food, our New Year's
gifts. But a certain Bishop of Angres, still haunted by pagan
sacrifice, maintained "that the cry *Au gui menez, Rollet Follet*,
was derived from the ancient Druids, who went out to cut
the *Gui* or Mistletoe, shouting and hollowing all the way,
and on bringing it from the woods the cry of old was *Au Gui
l'an neuf, le Roi vient*." As our author sagely remarks, "although
we must not suppose that the Druids spoke French, we may
easily allow the cry to have become changed with the language,
while the custom continued." But this, as the editors of the
Dictionary of Folklore most seriously remark, "attributes to
popular custom more historical continuity than one has reason
to expect."

None the less Skeat was willing to accept that "if the French phrase *au gui menez* is genuine, the derivation of Hogmanay from it is nearly certain . . . and all speculation as to the origin of the word *gui* may be spared; for it is neither Celtic nor Scandinavian, but simply the French spelling of Latin *uiscum* (or *viscum*), mistletoe." If it is genuine. Alas, the *OED* has no doubt, for "the alleged French cry cited in Jamieson is not to be found in the French author from whom it professes to be quoted, and appears as a figment."

However, we are still left with the Bishop's strange phrase *Au guy l'an neuf.* This Cotgrave in 1611 translates "To the mistletoe, the New Year" and calls it "the voice of countrey people begging small presents, or new-yeare's gifts, in Christmas." He too is very definite about its history, assuring his readers it is "an ancient tearme of rejoicing, derived from the Druids; who were wont, the first of January, to goe unto the woods, where having sacrificed and banqueted together, they gathered Mistletoe, esteeming it excellent to make beasts fruitful, and most soveraigne against all poison."

Selden, a little later, reiterates this, though rather more doubtfully. "On this Druidian custom," he says, "some have grounded that unto this day used in France, where the younger country fellows about New Yeare's tide, in every village, give the wish of good fortune at the inhabitants dores, with this acclamation, *Au guy, l'an neuf*, i.e., to the mistletoe this New Year: which I remember, in Rablais is read all one word for the same purpose." Now the phrase he remembered from Rabelais was *aller à l'aguillanneuf*, translated by Sir Thomas Urquhart as "to go a handsel-getting on the first day of the New Year".

That this translation is accurate is confirmed by Souchet, who noted that "with us (in La Beaune) people go on New Year's day to their relatives' and friends' houses, to solicit gifts, vulgarly called *l'eguilanleu.*" Brand records the same custom and quotes what purports to be a song sung by "countrey people" at this time:

Aguilaneuf de céans,[1]
On le voit à sa fenêtre
Avec son petit bonnet blanc,
Il dit qu'il sera Maître,
Mettera le pot au feu;
Donnez nous, ma bonne dame,
Donnez nous Aguilaneuf.

And in fact, confirms the *OED*, *aguillanneuf* "corresponds exactly in sense and use" to the Scottish Hogmanay, meaning as it does "the last day of the year, new year's gift, the festival at which new year's gifts were given and asked with the shout of *aguillanneuf*." Like Hogmanay, too, it occurs in innumerable different spellings, among them such odd variations as *haguilennef, haguimenlo, hoguignettes, haguirenleux* and so on. But in Normandy the local form was usually *hoguinanno* or *hoguimane*.

At last, then, we have found the origin of Hogmanay. But mystery still remains, for no one can be certain what *aguillanneuf* really means. "The second element," remarks the *Scottish National Dictionary* succinctly, "appears to be *l'an neuf. Agui* is obscure." Experts agree only that it doesn't relate to mistletoe; "these explanations . . . are now rejected by French scholars as merely popular etymology." So much for romance. The one other suggested derivation I have found is from Partridge, who thinks *gui* might stand for *huic*, dative of *hic—à huic l'an neuf*, to this New Year. But none of the commonest spellings supports this bastard form.

It must be hurtful to Scottish pride to discover that haggis is English and Hogmanay French, most probably borrowed round about 1560 and owing its introduction to the Auld Alliance.

[1] *ici dedans*, here within.

Yet even here all is not as simple as it sounds. Not surprisingly Spanish has a similar word with a similar meaning, *aguinaldo* or *aguilando*. One suggestion is that this might be a corruption of Latin *calendae*, the Calends, the first day of the month. And the Gaelic name for this season is *Oidhche Chaluinne*, *oidhche* meaning night or eve, and *chaluinne* or *caluinn* the New Year, derived quite definitely this time from Latin *calendae*.

Finally, what of Trololay? About this there is no secret. It is simply "a refrain of a song, expressing careless gaiety or jollity", occurring in many versions from the medieval "Hey! trolly lolly!" to the more modern "Tol de rol" or even "Tra la la". Quite why a cheerful man makes this noise no one can say; he has certainly been doing it for centuries. In the Chester Plays where a song is required from the Shepherds there is a direction, "Singe troly loly, troly loe". And in *Piers Plowman* Piers himself, asked to lead the pilgrims to Saint Truth, tells them he cannot, since he has a half-acre to plough. Anxious for his company, everyone lends a hand:

> Dikeres and delverers digged up the balkes . . .
> Eche man in his manere made hym-self to done,
> And some to plese Perkyn piked up the wedes.

But not all of them were so helpful:

> And thanne seten somme and songen atte nale,
> And hulpen erie his half acre with "how! trolli-lolli!"

Which means, as Skeat explains, that "all which some of the men did towards ploughing the half acre was to sit and sing choruses over their cups."

Yet even now we haven't escaped from the Druids. Nor from Dr. Charles Mackay. He had a theory that this and other similar refrains, "the Fal lal la, the Tra la la, the Fa lero loo, the Tooral-looral, the Derry down, derry down, the Tire lire, and other apparently absurb collections of syllables . . . are all relics of the once solemn worship by the Druids of the Sun and the heavenly bodies." Clearly such now unintelligible words were once part of hymns to the rising sun, "sung by thousands of deep-voiced priests marching in solemn procession . . . to salute with music and song and reverential homage the rising of the glorious orb which cheers and fertilizes the world." Because of our lack of understanding these great hymns have now "wholly departed from the recollection of men and (their) poor dishonoured relics are spoken of by scholars and philosophers as trash, gibberish, nonsense, and an idle farago of sounds, of no more philological value than the lowing of cattle or the bleating of sheep."

It is indeed a solemn thought. And his explanations are so ingenious the fact that they are, to say the least, unreliable scarcely matters. Trololay, or in his version "High trolollie, lollie, lol", he interprets as "the Gaelic *Ai!* or *Aibhe!*, Hail! or All Hail! *Trath*, pronounced *trah*, early, and *là*, day! or *Ai, tra là, là, là*—Hail, early day!, a chorus which Moses and Aaron may have heard in the temples of Egypt, when the priests saluted the rising sun as he beamed upon the grateful world"—the Celts being Asiatics and descended from the Ancient Egyptians, among others.

After this it seems almost invidious to remark that at one time, according to Grose, trolly lolly was a cant term for "coarse lace once much in fashion". Whether this implies that it was "a piece of nonsense" I do not know.

In all this there is little to support the average Englishman's idea of Hogmanay—kilted Scotsmen dancing and drinking and singing Auld Lang Syne. But we are dealing with centuries; this now indispensable song did not become so till about 1800. And even by 1790 there was a modern ring to the celebrations. For "on the last night of the old year (peculiarly called Hagmenai), the visitors and company made a point of not separating till after the clock struck twelve, when they rose, and, mutually kissing, wished each other a happy New Year."

ACKNOWLEDGEMENTS

I acknowledge my gratitude to the following for permission to quote from copyright material:

The Clarendon Press, Oxford, for *The Oxford English Dictionary* (12 vols), *An Etymological Dictionary of the English Language* by W. W. Skeat, *The Oxford Dictionary of Nursery Rhymes* and *The Lore and Language of School Children* by I. and P. Opie.

Cassell and Co. Ltd., for Brewer's *Dictionary of Phrase and Fable* by E. Cobham Brewer (1923 edition).

Routledge and Kegan Paul Ltd., for *Origins* by Eric Partridge.

The Folk-lore Society, London, for *British Calendar Customs* by A. R. Wright and *British Calendar Customs, Scotland,* by M. Macleod Banks.

T. and T. Clark, Edinburgh, for *The Encyclopaedia of Religion and Ethics*, edited by James Hastings.

Funk and Wagnalls Co., New York, for *The Dictionary of Folklore, Mythology and Legend*, edited by M. Leach and J. Fried.

G. and C. Merriam, Co., publishers of the Merriam–Webster Dictionaries, for Webster's *Third New International Dictionary* 1961.

G.E.

INDEX